SETTING THE RECORD STRAIGHT
MORMONS & HOMOSEXUALITY

SETTING THE RECORD STRAIGHT
MORMONS & HOMOSEXUALITY

A. Dean Byrd, Ph.D., MPH

Millennial Press, Inc.
P.O. Box 1741
Orem, UT 84059

ISBN: 1-932597-44-1

Copyright © 2008 Millennial Press

Cover design and typesetting by Adam Riggs

Dedication

To those men who have allowed me to accompany them on their journey out of homosexuality. I am forever grateful. Their voices are many and their message is singular and clear: we do exist.

Contents

Introduction

In the 1970s, I was a newly minted psychologist and a university-trained social scientist, working in metropolitan Washington, D.C. I managed both a clinical practice as well as academic appointments. For reasons not clear to me, a substantial minority of my patients were men who were unhappy with their homosexual attractions. About half of these men were married, had children, and complained of unwanted homosexual attraction in their lives. They professed love for their wives and families, had considered becoming involved sexually with other men, but had decided they wanted help in diminishing homosexual attraction and increasing their heterosexual potential. The other half of these men were single, in their mid-thirties, and equally as unhappy with their homosexual struggles. They had lived the "lifestyle" and found little joy. Their complaint, "Homosexuality is not working for me," was followed by the question, "Can you help me explore my options?" All of these men were depressed, many had addictions of one kind or another, and some were even suicidal.

Though gay activism was beginning to emerge within the national mental health organizations, it was still permissible to treat those individuals whose homosexuality was "ego-dystonic." Translated, this simply meant that if homosexual attraction was distressful to individuals, they certainly had the right to receive psychological care aimed at diminishing or eliminating

1

those unwanted attractions. However, even in the 70s, many mental health professionals were wary of gay activism and the politics of intimidation and exercised extreme care in any kind of advertisement about such professional services. I was one of those professionals, a typical psychologist who avoided any unpleasantness. I simply provided the psychological care consistent with the requests from my patients.

Though some of my patients who struggled with unwanted homosexual attraction were challenging, most were motivated and worked very hard. The therapeutic outcomes were similar to the outcomes for other difficult challenges. Many individuals were able to eliminate or significantly diminish homosexual attractions and make changes in their lives. A good majority made significant improvement, and they were bothered only slightly or not at all by such attractions. Most all of these men reported improved mental health and virtually no depression (depression, I learned, often accompanied the unwanted homosexual attraction) and seemed overall much happier. Follow-up for these individuals, some for as many as twenty-five years, revealed that the changes had been sustained.

My reputation for working with this population spread by word of mouth, and soon I found myself on the national scene. Though the state and national organizations did not seem particularly happy that I was helping those distressed with their homosexual attractions, there were no complaints. In fact, in almost four decades of practice, I have never had a single complaint lodged against my license for providing reorientation therapy (or for any other reason, for that matter).

By the late 80s, HIV/AIDS had emerged as a significant public health problem, and I began treating these men for both unwanted homosexual attractions as well as for the distress associated with HIV/AIDS. I was amazed to discover that my patients did well with both the unwanted homosexual attraction as well as the difficulties associated with this horrific disease. Interesting enough, many of these men found much comfort in reconnecting with their families of origin and the faith tradition of their childhood. To them, homosexuality and HIV/AIDS had more than just medical and psychological consequences. There were spiritual ramifications.

It was during this time that I had an epiphany myself: I first realized that with virtually every man to whom I had provided psychological care, his success seemed associated with some kind of spiritual experience—a kind of a discovery about his true nature. Indeed the philosopher Pierre Teilhard de Chardin seemed to have it right: "We are not human beings having a spiritual experience. We are spiritual beings having a human experience."

It was this sense of spiritual self as being male or female, accompanied by roles that were not just culturally defined but divinely designed, that had been derailed through a myriad of mortal events. These traumas, many of which had originated quite early in their lives, had left these men alone and confused about their gender and led them into a lifestyle that had not remedied their distress but rather had worsened their struggle. Indeed, for many, it was the discovery of their true selves that brought comfort, peace, and joy amidst the storms of difficulties. Challenges seemed harder to sort out in a secular world that offered so little hope and that was filled with so much activism.

Chronology

Secular Chronology

1973

Propelled by gay activism, Dr. Robert L. Spitzer leads the charge to remove homosexuality from the psychiatric manual. The diagnosis is replaced with "ego-dystonic homosexuality," meaning that if homosexual attractions were distressful to the patient, he or she had the right to psychological care.

1974

The American Psychological Association follows suite and the ensuing effort to support the removal of diagnosis is led by Dr. Nicholas A. Cummings. Support of the removal from the psychiatric manual carries with it the stipulation that research will be conducted to justify the removal. No such research is ever done.

1986

The U.S. Supreme Court upholds a Georgia law banning sodomy between consenting adults.

1987

Ego-dystonic homosexuality is removed from the revised psychiatric manual.

1993

Hawaii Supreme Court rules that the state constitution could give gay couples the same marital rights as heterosexual couples.

1996

President Clinton signs the Defense of Marriage Act, which defines marriage as a union of one man and one woman. It says states need not recognize same-sex marriages from other states.

1998

Hawaii voters amend state constitution, allowing legislature to reserve marriage for opposite-sex couples.

2000

Vermont becomes the first state to allow civil unions between same-sex partners, giving them most of the benefits of marriage.

2003

Dr. Robert L. Spitzer's study is published in the *Archives of Sexual Behavior*. Based on his research, Spitzer concludes that homosexuality is not invariably fixed in all people.

2003

U.S. Supreme Court strikes down a Texas law barring consensual gay sex, thus reversing its 1986 decision. Massachusetts Supreme Judicial Court rules that same-sex couples have a right to marry.

2004

The American Psychological Association passes resolutions supporting homosexual marriage and adoption by homosexual couples.

2006

The New York Court of Appeals, the state's highest court, rejects gay marriage, as does the Washington Supreme Court. The New Jersey Supreme Court rules gay couples have the same rights as heterosexual couples. It lets the legislature decide whether to allow same-sex marriage or civil unions.

2007

The Maryland Court of Appeals, the state's highest court, upholds the ban on gay marriage.

2008

The California Supreme Court strikes down a state ban on same-sex marriage.

Church Chronology

1969

"Crime Against Nature" is published as chapter 6 in Spencer W. Kimball's *The Miracle of Forgiveness*.

1971

President Spencer W. Kimball authors the *A Letter to a Friend* pamphlet.

1978

Elder Boyd K. Packer authors the *To the One* pamphlet.

1980

In a "Special Message to All Latter-day Saints," President Kimball speaks out on morality. See *Ensign* (November 1980): 94–98.

1988

The First Presidency issues a statement on AIDS.

1990

For the Strength of Youth pamphlet is released.

1991

The First Presidency Statement on Standards of Morality and Fidelity is released.

1994

The First Presidency Statement on Same-Gender Marriage is released.

1995

President James E. Faust authors the First Presidency message entitled "Serving the Lord and Resisting the Devil." See *Ensign* (November 1995): 3.

"Same-Gender Attraction" by Elder Dallin H. Oaks is published in the *Ensign*. See *Ensign* (October 1995): 7.

President Gordon B. Hinckley reads "The Family: A Proclamation to the World" as part of his message to the Relief Society.

1997

Teachings of Gordon B. Hinckley is published by Deseret Book. It reads: "Prophets of God have taught through the ages that practices of homosexual relations, fornication, and adultery are grievous sins. Sexual relations outside the bonds of marriage are forbidden by the Lord. We affirm those teachings."

1998

Gordon B. Hinckley authors "What Are People Asking About Us?" which reads: "People inquire about our position on those who consider themselves so-called gays and lesbians. . . . We love them as sons and daughters of God. They may have certain inclinations which are powerful and which may be very difficult to control. . . . If they do not act on these inclinations, then they can go forward as do all other members of the Church. If they violate the law of chastity and the moral standards of the Church, then they are subject to the discipline of the Church, just as others are." See *Ensign* (November 1998): 70.

Church donates $1.1 million in support of proposed constitutional amendment protecting traditional marriage in Alaska and Hawaii.

2000

Church leaders ask members to support California Proposition 22 in defense of marriage.

Elder Boyd K. Packer authors "Ye are the Temple of God," which reads, "The scriptures plainly condemn those who 'dishonor their own bodies between themselves . . . ; men with men working that which is unseemly,' or 'women [who] change the natural use into that which is against nature' . . . We do not reject you . . . only immoral behavior." See *Ensign* (November 2000): 72.

2001

For the Strength of Youth pamphlet reads, "Homosexual activity is a serious sin."

2004

True to the Faith booklet reads, "Like other violations of the law of chastity, homosexual activity is serious sin. It is contrary to the purposes of human sexuality (see Romans 1:24–31). It distorts loving relationships and prevents people from receiving the blessings that can be found in family life and the saving ordinance of the gospel."

Statement is issued by the First Presidency on Same-Gender Marriage, which, in part, reads, "Homosexual, including lesbian behavior, is a deviation from divine law in any age regardless of its private toleration, popular promotion, or legal sanction. Society may redefine deviation, but God has not repealed his commandments."

Church supports Utah's constitutional amendment defining marriage between a man and a woman. The First Presidency statement reads, "The Church of Jesus Christ of Latter-day Saints favors a constitutional amendment preserving marriage as lawful union of a man and a woman."

2006

"Same-Gender Attraction," an interview with Elder Dallin H. Oaks and Elder Lance B. Wickman, is released. "Homosexual behavior is and always will remain before the Lord an abominable sin."

The First Presidency sends letter to priesthood leaders urging support of a federal constitutional amendment defining marriage between a man and a woman.

On behalf of The Church of Jesus Christ of Latter-day Saints, Elder Russell M. Nelson joins the Religious Coalition on Marriage. Issues Letter on Federal Marriage Amendment (May, 25).

2007

Elder Jeffrey R. Holland authors "Helping Those Who Struggle with Same-Gender Attraction." See *Ensign* (October 2007): 42.

The Church of Jesus Christ of Latter-day Saints joins the California Catholic Conference, the National Association of Evangelicals, and the Union of Orthodox Jewish Congregations of America in an *amici curiae* brief supporting marriage between a marriage and a woman.

2008

The Church issues a statement in response to the California Supreme Court decision to allow homosexual marriage: "The Church of Jesus Christ of Latter-day Saints recognizes that same-sex marriage can be an emotional and divisive issue. However, the church teaches marriage between a man and a woman is ordained of God and that the family is the basic unit of society. Yesterday's California Supreme Court Decision is unfortunate."

Questions
and Answers

What is homosexuality?

Homosexuality is simply defined as sexual preference for one's own sex.

What causes homosexuality?

There is no consensus among scientists as to what causes homosexuality. Recently, the American Psychological Association issued a statement indicating that most scientists think homosexuality is caused by "a complex combination of nature and nurture."[1] It is likely that there are many roads that lead into (and out of) homosexuality.

Is there a gay gene?

No. The researchers whose studies have attempted to find biological causes for homosexuality have all admitted that they failed. After reviewing the research on homosexuality, Dr. Francis S. Collins, the director of the Human Genome Project, concluded that homosexuality is "genetically influenced but not hardwired by DNA and that whatever genes are involved represent predispositions, not predeterminations."[2] Interestingly enough, one could make this statement about most difficult challenges.

Why did the American Psychiatric Association remove homosexuality from its list of mental disorders?

Activist researcher and self-identified homosexual Simon LeVay concluded, "Gay activism was clearly the force that propelled the American Psychiatric Association to declassify homosexuality."[3]

Why is there so much interest in portraying homosexuality as something that is inborn?

People who think that homosexuals are born that way are more likely to support gay rights. Though there is no science to support the notion that homosexuality is inborn, the gay activists in the mental health organizations as well as in the media still continue to trumpet the "born that way" notion. A prominent lesbian psychologist makes the following statement, "It may be that for now, the safest way to advocate for lesbian/gay/bisexual rights is to keep propagating a deterministic model: sexual minorities are born that way and can never be otherwise. If this is an easier route to acceptance (which may in fact be the case), is it really so bad that it is inaccurate?"[4]

Are there different degrees of homosexuality?

There is a tendency to fuse three terms: homosexual attraction, homosexual orientation, and homosexual identity. Homosexual attractions are basically defined as erotic or sexual feelings toward members of one's own sex. These feelings may or may not persist. Homosexual orientation involves overall feelings of arousal toward members of one's own sex that includes both emotional and sexual components. Homosexual identity is a social/political label that one constructs to define one's self.

Once established, is homosexuality changeable?

There is clear and compelling evidence that homosexuality is more fluid than fixed and that indeed some people can make changes in their lives. In his study of whether self-identified homosexuals could change their orientation to heterosexual, Dr. Robert L. Spitzer, who ironically was the psychiatrist who led the effort for the American Psychiatric Association to delete homosexuality from the psychiatric manual, concluded that change was indeed possible for some people. Though skeptical when he began his study, Spitzer concluded, "Like most psychiatrists, I thought that homosexual behavior could be resisted, but sexual orientation could not be changed. I now believe that is untrue—some people can and do change."[5]

What is the prevalence of homosexuality in the general population?

Research has consistently determined that from 2 to 4 percent of the population is homosexual.[6]

What do researchers say about homosexuality and mental illness?

Several researchers have concluded that those who engage in homosexual practices are at risk for mental illnesses including depression, anxiety, and even suicidality. While there have been some activist attempts to suggest that society's lack of acceptance causes mental distress, this does not appear to be supported. Even when research is conducted in gay-affirming societies like the Netherlands, the conclusions are the same.[7]

Does having homosexual challenges preclude individuals from serving in the Church?

No. President Gordon B. Hinckley stated, "Most people have inclinations of one kind or another at various times. If they do not act upon these inclinations, then they can go forward as do all other members of the Church."[8]

What exactly is the Church's position on homosexuality?

The Church's position on homosexuality was beautifully articulated in an interview with Elder Dallin H. Oaks and Elder Lance B. Wickman: "Homosexual behavior is and always will remain before the Lord an abominable sin."[9] Elder Oaks further explains, "There is no fullness of joy in the next life without a family unit, including a husband, a wife, and posterity. Further, men are that they might have joy. In the eternal perspective, same-gender activity will only bring sorrow and grief and the loss of eternal opportunities."[10]

Should members with homosexual challenges be encouraged to marry?

Elder Oaks offered the following response to that question: Quoting President Hinckley, Elder Oaks stated, "'Marriage should not be viewed as a therapeutic step to solve problems such as homosexual inclinations or practices.' . . . Persons who have this kind of challenge that they cannot control could not enter marriage in good faith. . . . On the other hand, persons who have cleansed themselves of any transgression and who have shown their ability to deal with these feelings or inclinations and put them in the background, and feel a great attraction for a daughter of God and therefore desire to enter marriage and have children and enjoy the blessings of eternity—that's a situation when marriage would be appropriate."[11]

What resources are available to help those who struggle with homosexual challenges?

The Church has a number of resources including a recent pamphlet entitled, "God Loveth His Children."[12] LDS Family Services and Evergreen International provide resources as well. There are a number of websites that are helpful such as PeopleCanChange.com and NARTH.com. Perhaps the best resources are family members and bishops.

What should family members do when a loved one reveals homosexual difficulties?

I wrote an article for the *Ensign* in 1999. It offers some useful helps for parents.[13]

Does the Church have a position on homosexual marriage?

The First Presidency issued a statement in 1994 that included the following: "The principles of the gospel and the sacred responsibilities given us require that The Church of Jesus Christ of Latter-day Saints oppose any efforts to give legal authorization to marriages between persons of the same gender."[14]

Does the Church favor a federal constitutional amendment defining marriage as the union of one man and one woman?

Yes.[15]

What should our attitudes be toward those individuals who are self-identified as gay and lesbian?

President Hinckley indicated that we "should love them as sons and daughters of God."[16] Elder Oaks noted, "Our doctrines obviously condemn those who engage in so-called 'gay-bashing'—physical or verbal attacks on persons thought to be involved in homosexual or lesbian behavior."[17]

What does the research say about the homosexuality and parenting?

There is a dearth of research on parenting by homosexual individuals and homosexual couples. Most of the research has been conducted on children who were conceived in a heterosexual relationship and whose mothers later identified as lesbian. The research that is available causes some concerns. For example, the research conducted by Judith Stacey and Timothy Biblarz concluded with the following: Lesbians have a feminizing effect on their sons and a masculinizing effect on their daughters. The bigger question is how healthy is the rejection of gender roles?[18]

Is child sexual abuse a factor in the development of homosexual attractions?

First of all, sexual abuse causes havoc in the lives of children and does have the potential of contributing to gender confusion. Some research does show that child sexual abuse is overrepresented in the histories of those who later identify as homosexual.[19]

If you could offer a summary statement in the area of homosexuality, what might that statement be?

First of all, I would say that it is important to understand what science can and cannot say about the genesis and treatment of unwanted homosexuality. Based on the scientific evidence, one can conclude that a "biopsychosocial model mediated by agency" best fits the data. That is, homosexuality emerges from a complex combination of biological factors such as temperament along with environmental factors such as those associated with sexual abuse and peer abuse as well as difficult parental relationships. We also must not forget the role of agency—there is choice in how we respond to any attractions, whether sexual or otherwise. Finally, there is good emerging evidence that homosexuality is more fluid than fixed and that psychological care can indeed help to diminish or eliminate unwanted homosexual attractions.

Notes

1. American Psychological Association (2008). Answers to Your Questions for a Better Understanding of Sexual Orientation and Homosexuality, Washington, D. C.
2. Collins, F. S. (2006). *The Language of God.* New York: Free Press, p. 260.
3. LeVay, S. (1996). *Queer Science.* Cambridge, Massachusetts: The MIT Press, p. 224.
4. Diamond, L. M. (2008). *Sexual Fluidity: Understanding Women's Love and Desire.* Cambridge, Massachusetts: Harvard University Press, p. 257.
5. NARTH Press Release (May 9, 2001). "Prominent Psychiatrist Announces New Study Results: Some Gays Can Change," Encino, California: www.narth.com. Also in Nicolosi, J. and Nicolosi, L. A. (2002) *A Parent's Guide to Preventing Homosexuality.* Downer's Grove, Illinois: Intervarsity Press, p. 140.
6. Collins, F S. (2006), IBID.
7. Herrell, R., Goldberg, J., True, W. R. , Ramakrishnan, V. , Lyons, M., Eisen, S. & Tsuang, M. T.. (1999). "Sexual orientation and suicidality, " *Archives of General Psychiatry*, 56, p. 867; Ferguson, D. M., Horwood, L. J. & Beautrais, A. L. (1999). "Is sexual orientation related to mental health problems and suicidality in young people?" *Archives of General Psychiatry*, 56, p. 876; Bailey, J. M. (1999). "Homosexuality and mental illness, " *Archives of General Psychiatry*, 56, p. 884; Sandfort, T G., de Graaf, R., Bijl, R. V, & Schnabel, P. (2001). "Same-sex behavior and psychiatric disorders, *Archives of General Psychiatry*, 58, p. 85.
8. Hinckley, G. B. (1998, November). "What are people asking about us?" *Ensign,* 28(11), p. 71.

9. The Church of Jesus Christ of Latter-day Saints (August 14, 2006). "Same-Gender Attraction."NEWSROOM. LDS. ORG. Downloaded from http://www.lds.org/newsroom/issues/answer/0,1949,16056-1-201-4-201,html on 8/21/2006.
10. IBID.
11. IBID.
12. "God Loveth His Children," (2007).Salt Lake City, Utah: The Church of Jesus Christ of Latter-day Saints – Intellectual Reserve.
13. Byrd, A. D. (September, 1999). "When a loved one struggles with same-sex attraction," *Ensign*, 29 (9) p. 51-55.
14. The Church of Jesus Christ of Latter-day Saints, Letter from The First Presidency, February 1, 1994.
15. The Church of Jesus Christ of Latter-day Saints, Letter from The First Presidency, May 25, 2006.
16. Hinckley, G. B. (1998). IBID.
17. Oaks, D. H. (October, 1995). "Same-Gender Attraction," *Ensign*, 25 (10), p.8.
18. Stacey, J. and Biblarz, T. J. (2001). "Does sexual orientation of parents matter?" *American Sociological Review*, 66, 2, p. 159-183.
19. Tomeo, M. E. , Templer, D.I., Anderson, S. & Kotler, D. (2001). "Comparative data of childhood and adolescent molestation in heterosexual and homosexual persons," *Archives of Sexual Behavior*, 30, 5, p.535-541.

Homosexuality and Gay Activism: A Brief History

Prior to 1973, homosexuality was listed as a mental disorder in the DSM (Diagnostic and Statistical Manual of the American Psychiatric Association). A great deal of activism was occurring within the national mental health organizations, particularly the American Psychiatric Association. Activists disrupted meetings of the association with their protests, claiming psychiatry was the enemy. The activists found their way onto panels at the national conventions, and, on one occasion, psychiatrist John Freyer appeared on an American Psychiatric Association panel as Dr. Anonymous. He was dressed in a rubber mask, wig, and oversized tuxedo as he discussed the victimization of homosexuals, comparing them to African Americans.[1] Such disruptions and presentations of victimhood were common and aimed at forcing the American Psychiatric Association to remove homosexuality from the diagnostic manual.

One young psychiatrist, Dr. Robert L. Spitzer, was a junior member of the American Psychiatric Association's committee assigned with the task of classifying mental disorders. At the insistence of some gay activists, Dr. Spitzer met with them. The activists persuaded Dr. Spitzer that to remove homosexuality from the psychiatric classification would remove the social stigma and prejudice that many of them had endured. Spitzer was quick to point out that to remove homosexuality as a mental disorder was not necessarily the same as saying that it was a normal variant of human sexuality. His intent was to minimize the social discrimination against homosexual men and women. Recognizing that he was going against the prevailing orthodoxy of the time, Spitzer was challenged by the chair of the task force to come up with some kind of proposal. He wrote a compromise proposal that was presented at the American Psychiatric Association annual meeting in Hawaii in 1973. Basically, it was a proposal saying that if homosexuals did not want help they should not be forced into treatment. However, if the homosexual attractions were distressful (ego-dystonic), they were entitled to psychological care. Specifically, ego-dystonic homosexuality would remain a mental disorder for which psychological care would be available.

With Spitzer's intervention and proposal on behalf of the gay activists, a firestorm erupted in the American Psychiatric Association. Intense opposition to the removal came from a few outspoken psychiatrists like Dr. Irving Bieber and Dr. Charles Socarides, who had been successfully treating homosexuals for many years. Yet, when these esteemed psychiatrists complained that science and clinical experience did not support the removal of homosexuality from the DSM, they were demonized and even threatened, rather than scientifically refuted.

The American Psychiatric Association House of Delegates sidestepped the controversy by putting the matter to a vote of the membership. By a vote of 5,854 to 3,810, homosexuality was eliminated as a diagnostic category from the psychiatric manual, making it the first time in the history of healthcare that a diagnosis was decided by popular vote rather than by scientific evidence.

Even gay activist Simon LeVay admitted that science did not support the removal of homosexuality from the diagnostic manual. He noted, "Gay activism was clearly the force that propelled the APA [American Psychiatric Association] to de-classify homosexuality."[2]

As the American Psychiatric Association goes, so goes the other mental health organizations. The American Psychological Association (APA) followed suite, and Dr. Nicholas Cummings was the spokesman. Dr. Cummings offered the resolution, declaring that homosexuality was not a psychiatric condition. However, the resolution carried with it a stipulation that appropriate research needed to be conducted to support the resolution. Dr. Cummings watched with dismay as no efforts were made to promote or even encourage such research.[3] In fact, the stipulation seems to have been removed from the official records of the American Psychological Association.

Unfortunately, both the American Psychiatric Association and the American Psychological Association had established precedents that medical and psychological diagnoses are subject to political fiat. Currently, diagnosis in psychology and psychiatry is cluttered with politically correct verbiage that seems to have taken precedence over scientific data and demonstrable professional experience.

What's even more disturbing is that national organizations are issuing statements and making resolutions on abortion, boxing, Zionism, the nuclear freeze, methods of interviewing terrorists, the Equal Rights Amendment, same-sex marriage, and adoption by same-sex couples. There is no science behind such proclamations. In fact the national associations have no more expertise in such matters than does the typical citizen. Such proclamations are simply activism masquerading as science.

Such activism continues to this day, particularly in regard to such controversial topics as homosexuality. In *Destructive Trends in Mental Health*, editors Dr. Rogers Wright and Dr. Nicholas Cummings (chapters were written by an academy award roster of world-class mental health experts) declared that "psychology, psychiatry, and social work have been captured by an ultra-liberal agenda."[4]

One of the editors of this volume noted that he and his co-author lived through the abominable McCarthy era and the Hollywood witch hunts; still, he noted that there was "not the insidious sense of intellectual intimidation that currently exists under political correctness."[5] He now says "political correctness tethers our intellect."[6]

Dr. Wright and Dr. Cummings cannot simply be dismissed as some fanatical, right-wing conservatives because they are self-identified as "lifelong liberal activists" and influential leaders of the American Psychological Association who vigorously oppose the illiberalism of their fellow psychologists. Dr. Wright is a past president of Division 12, founding president of Division 31, founding president of the Council for the Advancement of the Psychological Professions and Science (CAPPS), a Fellow of APA, a diplomate in clinical psychology, the recipient of an honorary doctorate, and a distinguished practitioner of the National Academies of Practice. Dr. Cummings is currently distinguished professor at the University of Nevada and president of the Cummings Foundation for Behavioral Health. He also chairs the boards of both the Nicholas and Dorothy Cummings Foundation and CareIntegra. He is past president of the American Psychological Association, past president of Division 12 and Division 29, and the recipient of five honorary doctorates for contributions to psychology, education, and the Greek classics. He is the recipient of psychology's gold medal for lifetime contributions to practice.

These prominent professionals, perhaps the most recognized names in both the American Psychological Association and the field of mental health professionals in general, provide compelling evidence of the many destructive trends in the mental health profession where science is distorted and diversity has been redefined as a kind of narrow politicism where differing worldviews are not only summarily dismissed, but the holders of such views are also actually punished. "Psychology and mental health," says Cummings "have veered away from scientific integrity and open inquiry, as well as from compassionate practice in which the welfare of the patient is paramount."[7]

Perhaps there is no more blatant example of such activism than that which appeared in a Harvard Press publication wherein a member of the American Psychological Association and a "prominent" member of the university community offered the following regarding the research on homosexuality: "...it may be that for now, the safest way to advocate for lesbian/gay/bisexual rights is to keep propagating a deterministic model: sexual minorities are born that way and can never be otherwise. If this is an easier route to acceptance (which may in fact be the case), is it really so bad that it is inaccurate?"[8] This psychologist and university professor suggests the Machiavellian idea that the ends justifies the means: science really does not matter as long as a particular agenda is furthered.

Though political correctness and gay activism make it difficult to separate fact from fiction regarding such topics as homosexuality, when the research is carefully reviewed, what science can and cannot say based on the data does emerge. Unfortunately, the mainstream media and even the national mental organizations continue to misrepresent and distort the science. There are scientists and mental health care practitioners who differ, but most don't speak out because of fear of ostracism and retaliation—even loss of advancement and tenure. Wright and Cummings noted that many esteemed colleagues refused to write chapters for their book because of such fears.[9] There are gay activist groups within the national associations who are officially recognized, and though they are small, they are very vocal. Discussions on topics such as homosexuality are only permitted if they address issues such as "civil rights" and pass the watchful eye of the gatekeepers.

There are a few scientists and mental health practitioners, however, who continue to call attention to the fact and fiction regarding the science of homosexuality and provide psychological care to those with unwanted homosexual attraction. Fortunately, the numbers of such professionals are increasing, and they are beginning to sort out what science can and cannot say about the genesis of homosexuality and the outcomes of treatment for this patient population.

Homosexuality and Science

The Biological Argument

The messages that emanate from the national mental health organizations and that have even been cited in court briefs tout the notion that homosexuality is so strongly compelled by biological factors that it is indelibly ingrained in a person's core identity and therefore is not amenable to modification or change. Many of these articles, though well written, do not reflect good science. In fact, the social advocacy of these articles would suggest a greater reliance on politics than on the scientific method.

More than half of the individuals who write such articles are either self-identified homosexuals or are on record as supportive of homosexual causes. Nonetheless, when confronted directly, many of these individuals reluctantly admit that their research does not support a simple biological model of homosexual causation (though many wish that it did). They seem content, for the most part, to allow the distortions and misinterpretations of their studies to go uncritically examined. In short, they don't seem to object to the media spin that often favors the gay agenda.

The initial research used to support the model of biological causation of homosexuality came from Simon LeVay, Dean Hamer, and the team of J. Michael Bailey and Richard Pillard.

Of the four researchers, three (LeVay, Hamer, and Pillard) are self-identified as gay.

At the time of his research, LeVay was a biological scientist at the Salk Institute in San Diego. He conducted research on the brains of two groups of men: homosexual men and presumed heterosexual men. With fairly small sample sizes (nineteen homosexual men and sixteen presumed heterosexual men), LeVay conducted a post-mortem examination focusing on a particular cluster of cells in the hypothalamus known as INAH-3. He reported that he had found subtle but significant differences between the brains of homosexual and heterosexual men. [10]

LeVay's research had a number of limitations. He had very little information about the sexual histories of the research participants. Some of the participants died of HIV/AIDs. Although there were differences between the two groups studied, some presumed heterosexual men had small nuclei in the critical area, and some homosexual men had nuclei large enough to be included in the normal heterosexual range.

Activists proclaimed, based on this one study, that the biological roots of homosexuality had been established, and the "born-that-way" argument was touted in major media outlets. Opposing views were, for the most part, silenced.

However, LeVay himself, when pressed, contradicted the media's interpretation of his research. In his own words, LeVay declared:

> But it is important to stress several limitations of the study. First, the observations were made on adults who had already been sexually active for a number of years. To make a real compelling case, one would have to show that these neuroanatomical differences existed early in life—preferably at birth. Without such data, there is always at least the theoretical possibility that the structural differences are actually the *result* of differences in sexual behavior—perhaps the "use it or lose

it" principle. Furthermore, even if the differences in the hypothalamus rise before birth, they might still come about from a variety of causes, including genetic differences, differences in stress exposure, and many others. It is possible that the development of the INAH-3 (and perhaps other brain regions) represent a "final common path" in the determination of sexual orientation, a path to which innumerable factors may contribute.[11]

Further quoting LeVay,

> Another limitation arises because most of the gay men whose brains I studied died of AIDS. Although I am confident that the small size of INAH-3 in these men was not an effect of the disease, there is always the possibility that gay men who died of AIDS are not representative of the entire population of gay men. For example, they might have a stronger preference for receptive anal intercourse, the major risk factor for acquiring HIV infection. Thus, if one wished, one could make an argument that structural differences in INAH-3 relate more to actual behavioral patterns of copulation than to sexual orientation as such. It will not be possible to settle this issue definitively until some method becomes available to measure the size of INAH-3 in living people who can be interviewed in detail about their sexuality.[12]

Finally, LeVay summarized his research results in the following way:

> It is important to stress what I didn't find. I did not prove that homosexuality was genetic, or find a genetic cause for being gay. I didn't show that gay men are born that way, the most common mistake people make in interpreting my work. Nor did I locate a gay center in the brain. INAH-3 is less likely to be the sole gay nucleus of the brain than a part of a chain of nuclei engaged in men and women's sexual behavior. . . . Since I looked at adult brains we don't know if the differences I found were there at birth, or if they appeared later.[13]

Of course, LeVay made these statements quietly and did not appear on television, complaining that his research had been misinterpreted.

As is so often the case, when research such as LeVay's is so horrifically distorted in media outlets and goes uncritically examined, the researcher himself is part of the story. LeVay's partner died of AIDS in 1990. During the time he was caring for his dying partner, LeVay decided to switch careers and abandon his study of the visual system. Instead, as part of the gay rights movement, he sought to find a biological basis for homosexuality. However, the media distortions of LeVay's research made the front page of virtually every mainstream paper. In his book, *Why Gender Matters*, Dr. Leonard Sax noted that no such coverage was provided for the subsequent reports that LeVay had made a mistake. More recent, more rigorous research using more accurate methods has failed to demonstrate any differences between the brains of homosexual and heterosexual men.[14]

Most scientists would have duplicated their findings or pursued further research to support or not support their claims. LeVay did not. It's interesting to note that LeVay has abandoned his brain research and has devoted himself to political activism on the part of the gay movement. He is the president of the West Hollywood Institute for Gay and Lesbian Education (WHIGLE), and, as of this date, his research has not been replicated. LeVay spends his time speaking on behalf of the gay and lesbian movement.

Studying identical twins is a popular way to determine the relative contribution of genetic factors to a particular trait. J. Michael Bailey and Richard Pillard studied gay male twins and found a 52 percent concordance rate for identical twins, which means that for every homosexual twin, the chances were about 50 percent that his twin would be homosexual.[15] The most fascinating question is that if there was something in the genetic code that made an individual homosexual and at least some of the twins studied had homosexual "coding," why did not all the identical twins become homosexual because identical twins have the same genetic endowment? What is interesting is that Bailey recruited his participants in gay venues, venues where participants often ascertained whether their participation in Bailey's study would help the gay movement. Bailey himself acknowledged the probable selection bias and noted that he recruited in venues where participants considered the sexual orientation of their twins before agreeing to participate.[16] Bailey conducted a second study using the Australian Twin Registry, which had an anonymous response format, making similar bias unlikely. From this study, Bailey reported a concordance of 20 percent to 37.5 percent, depending on how loosely you define homosexuality.[17] The first study received a great deal of press. Bailey's second study received almost no media attention.

Though Bailey is hopeful for a biological basis for homosexuality, his research far from proves that homosexuality is inherited. In fact, he has even suggested that "homosexuality may represent a developmental error."[18] Noting the activism that seems to overshadow good research in this area, Bailey stated, "It would be a shame if sociopolitical concerns prevented researchers from conscientious consideration of any reasonable hypothesis."[19]

Regarding twin studies in general, it might be interesting to examine the available evidence for other traits. For example, the following statistics indicate genetic contributions to personality based on twin studies: general cognitive ability (50 percent); extroversion (54 percent); conscientiousness (49 percent); neuroticism (48 percent); openness (57 percent); aggression (38 percent); and traditionalism (54 percent).[20]

If anything, the twin research on homosexuality supports the role of the environment in determining whatever biological predispositions might be expressed. Indeed, that the environment can even modify gene expression is a fact of science.

The only conclusion that can be reached from the twin studies on homosexuality (and other characteristics) is that environmental influences play a strong role in the development of homosexuality (and other traits)!

The third study and perhaps the most sensationalized of the studies to advocate a biological basis for homosexuality emerged during the national discussion of gays in the military during the Clinton era. The study was conducted by a self-identified gay man, Dean Hamer, who was a senior scientist at the National Cancer Institute in Washington, D. C., and who did not initially disclose that he was gay.

Hamer and his group attempted to link male homosexuality to a stretch of DNA located at the tip of the X chromosome, the chromosome that some men inherit from their mothers. In Hamer's study, he examined forty pairs of non-identical twin, gay brothers and asserted that thirty-three pairs—a number significantly higher than the twenty pairs that chance would dictate—had inherited the same X-linked genetic markers from their mothers.[21]

Criticism of Hamer's research came from a surprising source: Dr. Neil Risch, the scientist at Yale University School of Medicine who invented the method used by Hamer. Risch commented, "Hamer *et al.* suggest that their results are consistent with X-linkage because maternal uncles have a higher rate of homosexual orientation than paternal uncles, and cousins related through a maternal aunt have a higher rate than other types of cousins. However, neither of these results are statistically significant."[22]

The media touted the discovery of the "gay" gene, and trumpeted that another study provided proof for the biological basis of homosexuality. Criticism of Hamer's study was not aired. Hamer, like LeVay, did little to correct the misinterpretation of his research. However, when questioned, he offered the following: "We knew genes were only part of the answer. We assumed the environment also played a role in sexual orientation, as it does in most, if not all behaviors."[23] Hamer further noted, "Homosexuality is not purely genetic . . . environment plays a role. There is not a single master gene that makes people gay. . . . I don't think we will ever be able to predict who will be gay."[24] Further, citing the failure of his own research in a book published later, Hamer concluded, "The pedigree failed to produce what we originally hoped to find: simple Mendelian inheritance. In fact, we never found a single family in which homosexuality was distributed in the obvious pattern that Mendel observed in his pea plants."[25]

What is even more intriguing is that when Hamer's study was replicated by George Rice *et al.*, with research that was more robust, the genetic markers were found to be nonsignificant. Rice *et al.* concluded, "It is unclear why our results are so discrepant from Hamer's original study. Because our study was larger than that of Hamer *et al.*'s, we certainly had adequate power to detect a genetic effect as large as reported in that study. Nonetheless, our data do not support the presence of a gene of large effect influencing sexual orientation at position XQ 28."[26]

All three researchers seemed content to allow the misinterpretation and misuse of their studies to continue in spite of the evidence to the contrary—presumably to support the gay agenda. Ethicality would demand they do otherwise. They continue to hope that a biological basis for homosexuality will be discovered. In response to my written criticism of one of the authors, he complained that I quoted him correctly but did not reflect his beliefs!

The biological studies have been extensively reviewed by world-renowned scientists such as William Byne and Bruce Parsons, and Richard Friedman and Jennifer Downey. Both of these exceptional research teams offered one conclusion: a simple biological model does not fit the current research.[27] In fact, Friedman and Downey concluded: "At clinical conferences one often hears . . . that homosexual orientation is fixed and immutable. Neither assertion is true. . . . The assertion that homosexuality is genetic is so reductionistic that it must be dismissed out of hand as a general principle of psychology."[28] Dr. Janet L. Cummings further noted, "The belief that homosexuality is always inbred flies in the face of available evidence that genetics, childhood environment, and personal choice are all factors. Granted, some may be more salient than others, but from the genetic standpoint alone, the genes responsible would have disappeared throughout the millennia from lack of reproductive activity."[29]

Perhaps the best succinct summary of the research on the genesis of homosexuality comes from Dr. Francis S. Collins, the head of the Human Genome Project at the National Institutes of Health. He offered the following:

> An area of particularly strong public interest is the genetic basis of homosexuality. Evidence from twin studies does in fact support the conclusion that heritable factors play a role in male homosexuality. However the likelihood that the identical twin of a homosexual male will also be gay is about 20% (compared with 2–4 percent of males in the general population), indicating that sexual orientation is genetically influenced but not hardwired by DNA, and that whatever genes are involved represent predispositions, not predeterminations.[30]

Dr. Collins went on to say that the environment, particularly childhood experiences as well as the role of free will, affect all of us in profound ways.[31]

In their recent book, *DNA: Promise and Peril*, genetic experts Linda and Edward McCabe concluded that even DNA sequence does not equal destiny. These scientists debunked the myths of genetic determinism and provided good evidence that the expression of genes is altered by experience.[32]

So why all the interest in proving that homosexuality is hardwired or that homosexuality is biologically determined? Perhaps LeVay has the answer. He noted that "people who think that gays and lesbians are 'born that way' are more likely to support gay rights."[33]

Homosexual fluidity is also a debate of interest. Lisa Diamond, a researcher, and member of the American Psychological Association and a gay activist, has concluded that sexual identity is far from fixed in women who are not exclusively heterosexual.[34] Although the researcher does not want her study, which clearly supports the fluidity of homosexuality, to be used to support the notion of fluidity, her longitudinal data does just that.[35]

Diamond is not alone in reaching the conclusion that homosexuality is more fluid than fixed, particularly in women. Ellen Schecter of the Fielding Graduate Institute conducted in-depth research with women who were self-identified as lesbian for more than ten years and had been in an ongoing heterosexual relationship for at least year. She concluded that labels such as "lesbian" may oversimplify women's sexual identity and experience.[36]

Sexual plasticity in homosexual men is not a new or novel idea. More than thirty years ago, Freund, using penile plethysmography, found that some homosexual men could voluntarily alter their penile responses to respond to heterosexual stimuli without ever receiving reorientation therapy.[37] Such scientific evidence, for the most part, remains buried in today's politically correct world.

With a few exceptions, the national organizations with their activist gatekeepers, continue to perpetuate the notion that homosexuality is simply a matter of biology though we are beginning to see some retreat.

Perhaps at least one national mental health association, the American Psychological Association, is beginning to realize that the scientific credibility of the organization is starting to erode because of providing false, misleading information on topics such as homosexuality. A dated document published by the American Psychological Association stated, "There is considerable recent evidence to suggest that biology, including genetic or inborn hormonal factors, play a significant role in a person's sexuality."[38] The more current document eliminated such statements and offered the following:

> There is no consensus among scientists about the exact reasons. . . . Although much research has examined the possible genetic, hormonal, developmental, social, and cultural influences on sexual orientation, no findings have emerged that permit scientists to conclude that sexual orientation is determined by any factor or set of factors. Many think that nature and nurture both play complex roles."[39]

Though there remains the reluctance to cite the studies that clearly demonstrate homosexuality is not simply a biological phenomenon, American Psychological Association has at least retreated to the extent that the leaders admit the research does not support a simple biological theory of homosexuality. Even the popular magazine *Mother Jones* featured an article titled, "Gay by Choice?" The author, who noted the mounting evidence that supported the malleability of homosexuality, wondered, "If science proves sexual orientation is more fluid than we have been led to believe, can homosexuality still be a protected right?" [40]

With the erosion of the biological argument, the nurture or psychological arguments are beginning to reemerge. Scientists and practitioners are beginning to recognize the complexity of homosexuality and to note that homosexuals are not a homogenous group. Many are beginning to recognize that there are likely many roads into and out of homosexuality and that homosexuality is, indeed, more fluid than once thought. Though there may be biological predispositions to homosexuality and other complex behaviors, the environment determines when and if those predispositions manifest themselves.

The Psychological Argument

Psychological theories of homosexuality can be basically placed into one of three categories: psychoanalytic, social learning, and interactional. Each has made contributions to understanding possible routes to developing homosexual attractions and homosexual behavior, and each is supported by some empirical evidence.

From a psychoanalytical perspective, homosexuality is rooted in difficult family relationships, particularly in a detached, disconnected father and an over-involved mother. Such unhealthy relationships contribute to the rejection of a masculine or feminine gender identity.[41]

There is some research to support the notion of disordered parent-child relationships where the child rejects identification with the same-sex parent and turns to same-sex peers or adults for love, support, and affirmation. For example, Alan Bell, Martin Weinberg, and Sue Hammersmith found that in their research 72 percent of the homosexual men recalled feeling very little or not at all like their fathers.[42] George Rekers concluded that the child's relationship to the father was predictive of the sexual identity outcome.[43] Research by Gregory Dickson *et al.* also found differences between mother-child relations when comparing homosexual men to heterosexual men.[44] However, psychoanalysis in general, and in this area in particular, suffers from rigorous studies to support this approach. Nonetheless, there is an abundance of case reports, particularly preceding 1973, that support this theory.

Social learning theory explains how we learn through actions, observations, and attitudes adopted from significant others. In this theory, both direct and indirect behavioral conditioning accounts for the attractions that we develop and the behaviors that we adopt. From this perspective, children and adolescents learn about sexual behavior and sexual preference from parents, peers, and media. They get rewarded or punished by significant others for their sexual attitudes or behaviors. A young boy, for example, may have been involved with masturbation activities with his peers and learned homosexual activity from such interactions. There is significant evidence to suggest that peers and the media have a tremendous influence on the sexual attitudes and behavior of adolescents in particular.

Social learning can also account for the role of serious trauma, such as sexual abuse, in the development of homosexual behavior. Some researchers have found a higher prevalence of sexual abuse in the histories of both male and female homosexuals. For example, Diane Shrier and Robert Johnson found that boys who were sexually abused were seven times more likely to self identify as homosexual or bisexual.[45] Richard Friedman and Jennifer Downey found that boys who later identified as homosexual became sexually active at a younger age than their heterosexual counterparts (12.7 years as opposed to 15.7 years).[46] Clinical histories of homosexual men provide evidence of such abuse. Consider the story of Olympic diver, self-identified homosexual, Greg Louganis as he describes being sexually abused by a man who was the same age as Greg's father:

> He put his arms around me and kissed me. I really liked being held, and I was thrilled that this guy found me attractive. . . . I thought over time that I would feel less ashamed about what I was doing, but it only got worse. The age difference bothered me more, and he couldn't exactly be a part of my life. I felt stupid telling him what I was doing at school and I couldn't introduce him to any of my classmates. I hated the separation and secrecy, but I kept going back for the affection, and he was happy to give it to me. . . . It upset me that he was so much older, not because I felt molested or anything. I had been more than a willing partner, but the differences in our ages made the experiences even more shameful.[47]

Greg further wrote, "At one point he told me he was concerned about seeing me because I was under eighteen. Apparently, he'd been jailed in the past for picking up minors."[48]

Sexual abuse creates havoc in the lives of children through the introduction of confusion, particularly gender confusion. Social learning theory explains how the affection and attention can be rewarding and how children can come to value such contact and develop an affinity for homosexual relationships based on physical stimulation. Such relationships, coupled with the notion that sexual activity can be reinforcing of itself, offers a plausible explanation for the development of homosexual attractions through the learning process. Boys, in particular, are prone to make such cognitive errors when sexual abusers have victimized them. They often interpret the physical stimulation associated with the sexual abuse as being evidence that they are homosexual. Boys don't seem to understand that the physical stimulation only evidences that their bodies are working; such abuse makes no judgment on the morality of the behavior.

Gender confusion is often found in the lives of homosexual men who were sexually abused as children.

There is evidence to support the role of peers in the development of homosexual attractions as well. In fact, the well-known psychiatrist Harry Stack Sullivan suggested that the lack of connections with same-sex peers set the stage for later development of homosexual attractions.[49] Peer neglect or peer abuse (teasing) often results in disconnections. Such trauma, particularly during the early pre-adolescent years, can cause gender confusion and subsequent problems with sexual orientation. More recently, support for the contributions of peer abuse to the development of homosexuality has come from the Pennsylvania psychiatrist Richard Fitzgibbons.[50]

It is important to understand that the data from many such studies is correlational, and no cause-and-effect conclusions can be drawn. Sexual abuse and peer abuse may be contributing factors to homosexual attractions and homosexual behaviors but do not directly cause the attractions. Such experiences often contribute to gender confusion and such confusion may actually make young boys vulnerable to a variety of challenges including homosexuality.

Interactional Theory

Interactional theory combines the indirect or predisposing effects of biology with the environmental theories to explain homosexuality. Daryl Bem, a self-identified gay researcher at Cornell University, postulated that genes do not directly cause homosexuality but rather set the stage for homosexuality by influencing temperament. His theory noted as EBE (Exotic Becomes the Erotic) suggests that temperament associated with gender non-conformity, where boys identify with girls and girls with boys in terms of their activities, prevents the child from interacting, bonding, or identifying with same-sex peers. Thus, during adolescence, these young people sexualize "otherness" or those with whom they are not identified. In other words, these pre-adolescents sexualize that with which they are not familiar. Bem's research is supportive of a developmental trajectory for homosexuality where boys, in particular, see themselves as different from their male peers, this difference becomes sexualized, and it later leads to the development of homosexual attractions.[51]

This interactional theory seems to be a logical alternative to either the biological, psychoanalytical, or social learning theories. The interaction theory postulates that biologically predisposed personality or temperament traits are nurtured in relationships and environmental contexts. Thus, this model accounts for a variety of factors, or what some have labeled the "conspiracy of factors," that later combine to shape homosexual attractions and behaviors. However, the primary drawback to this theory is the failure to consider the role of agency and choice in the development of homosexuality.

Agency and Homosexual Behavior: A Neglected Area

Biological theory suggests the force of nature (genes, prenatal hormones) is responsible for the development of homosexual attractions and behavior; environment suggests the influence of family and peer relationships, the importance of modeling, and the media; and the interactional model posits some contribution from each. However, what is the role of agency and choice or the person's own participation in the development of sexual preference?

Choice does not necessarily mean conscious choice. Sexual attractions are not necessarily chosen but responses to those attractions do involve choice. Unbidden attractions may come because of situational factors and prior personal experiences. There may even be some kind of biological predisposition that makes such attractions more probable than not, but these attractions may be increased or decreased by the choices that people make.

Byne and Parsons made this argument: "Conspicuously absent from most theorizing on the origins of sexual orientation is an active role of the individual in constructing his or her own [sexual] identity."[52] In 1998, Milton Diamond as well noted that while biology may predispose a person's sexual orientation, an individual is flexible in responding to such biological predispositions and environmental influences.[53] Perhaps the lesbian activist Camille Paglia said it best when she concluded: "There is an element of choice in all behavior, sexual or otherwise."[54]

Richard Williams added a different dimension to the notion of choice. He posited a two-fold process where there must be knowledge of truth accompanied by a decision to live truthfully.[55] Accordingly, agency consists of not just doing what we want to do but includes doing what we should do.

If we are indeed free to choose, there must be choices. In some cases of homosexuality, there may be no identified antecedents such as adverse life events, no abuse, no difficult parental or peer relationships, no identifiable cause. No one knows how he or she has arrived at homosexual attractions. The answer is quite complex, suggesting that simplistic models don't do justice to the topic. Research has pointed to possible biological factors, possible psychological factors, and the role of agency in the genesis of homosexuality. The interactionist model accompanied by individual choice in responding to these contributions is the more likely scenario.

A Biopsychosocial Model Mediated by Agency Best Fits the Data

The biopsychosocial model mediated by choice best represents the current state of the research on homosexuality. Homosexuality is not explained by either a simple biological model or a simple psychological model, and it cannot be reduced to a matter of conscious choice. There is emerging evidence to support the notion that homosexuality is not easily or simply defined, and there are qualitative differences among those who have homosexual attraction, who have a homosexual orientation, or who claim a homosexual identity. In other words, there are likely many roads that lead into (and out of) homosexuality. The most likely explanation is that homosexuality results from a complex combination of biological factors such as temperament and environmental traumas such as those associated with sexual or peer abuse along with difficult parental relationships. The combination is likely different for different people. We also must not forget that agency or choice in response to such attractions is always a factor whether the behavior is sexual or otherwise.

Perhaps a more important question is that once established, are homosexual attractions modifiable or changeable? Can an individual who is predominantly homosexual become heterosexual?

Psychological Care for Unwanted Homosexual Attraction: A Brief History

Prior to 1973, homosexuality was considered a mental illness and was treated through psychological care in much the same way as other mental illnesses. Though homosexuality was removed from the diagnostic manual in 1973, it was still permissible to provide psychological care if the individual was distressed by unwanted homosexual attractions (in other words, if their homosexual attractions were ego-dystonic). With the ever-present activism, however, even this caveat was removed in 1987 when ego-dystonic homosexuality was also deleted from the diagnostic manual and replaced with an innocuous category of those who were distressed by their sexual orientation without any mention of homosexuality (DSM 302.9 Sexual Disorder Not Otherwise Specified, 3. Persistent and marked distress about sexual orientation).

However, the activists continued their assault on the national organizations by suggesting that any desire for psychological care emerged from "internalized homophobia," an invented term used to intimidate both those who sought care as well as the providers of that care. A phobia, a legitimate diagnosis, is an irrational fear often accompanied by a set of distinct, physical symptoms toward the feared object. Activists co-opted the phobia terminology and used it to apply to anyone who disagreed with the gay agenda to legitimatize homosexual relationships. Thus individuals and institutions, particularly religious institutions, were labeled homophobic. Activists define homophobia as the internalized sense of self-hatred or self dis-like. This name-calling is used not only to prevent discussion of homosexuality but also to suggest to individuals seeking care for unwanted homosexual attraction that their motivation for seeking care is because they don't value themselves. That is, those unhappy with unwanted homosexuality really don't seek care for rational reasons but because they simply can't accept their inevitable, immutable homosexuality. Thus even seeking psychological care for unwanted homosexuality is held in sus-pect. Why would anyone seek care for homosexuality when it is no cause for alarm or distress? Activists claim it is rather a homophobic society that does not allow for the acceptance and expression of homosexuality that really causes distress in the individual!

This 1973 decision had a chilling effect on research on the causes of homosexuality as well as research on therapies designed to change homosexual attractions and discouraged professionals from publicly declaring that they would provide such care. Although psychological care continued and yielded results similar to those found in patients dealing with other difficult challenges, political correctness began to emerge and actually prevented the open discussion of providing care for unwanted homosexuality. That is, activists entered the profes-sional organizations and exerted undue influence on policies and resolutions as they perpetuated the view that homosexual-ity was like race and deserved federal and state protection. They reasoned if they could convince a fair-minded American public that homosexuality was an innate and immutable trait, they would be able to gain status as a protected group. That some people do change did not fit well with this political agenda. Concerted efforts were being made to declare the treatment of unwanted homosexuality unethical, even if individuals wanted to pursue such care. The national organizations were persuaded or intimidated into making such "scientific-sounding" statements and passing resolutions consistent with the gay agenda in direct violation of their own policies.

One such policy routinely violated by the American Psychological Association is the Leona Tyler Principle, which was formally adopted and never rescinded. This principle states that advocacy by the association should be based upon scientific data and demonstrable professional experience, leaving individual psychologists or groups free to advocate as concerned citizens. Dr. Leona Tyler, former president of the APA, sought to keep it a scientific organization and to prevent the organization from taking positions for which there was a dearth of scientific data. Other presidents of the American Psychological Association such as Dr. Nicholas Cummings, regularly prevented motions lacking scientific data from coming to the floor when the board of directors convened.[56] Today this principle is virtually ignored. Indeed, current presidents don't seem familiar with the principle, and evidence that it is violated is plentiful.

Even under circumstances where political correctness reigns, what the agenda-driven ideologues did not count on was the number of professionals who supported the civil rights of self-identified homosexuals but objected to the national organizations taking positions for which there was inadequate science and professional experience. These professionals deemed that an individual had a right to psychological care and that providers had a right to provide that care. They reasoned, rightly so, that client autonomy and client self-determination represented cornerstones of all psychological care, and they rejected the notion that such care was motivated by internalized homophobia. Rather these professionals reasoned that those unhappy with homosexual attractions could make rational decisions to seek psychological care to diminish or eliminate those attractions and develop their heterosexual potential. Many of these professionals had been quietly providing this care with outcomes not so dissimilar to other mental health challenges. These professionals exist in virtually every venue from the schools to the hospitals to state and federal agencies. They are fully licensed to provide psychological care and have been quiet observers of the erosion of science in the mental health organizations while at the same time providing care for those with unwanted homosexual attractions and documenting their successes. Being forced into the academic and professional closets, they nonetheless continued to provide effective, ethical care for individuals with unwanted homosexual attractions. Some networking was ongoing but many of these professionals worked in isolation and were not connected to other professionals until in the early 90s.

It was in 1992 that these professionals met in New York City and organized themselves into a vibrant organization committed to research and psychological care for those with unwanted homosexual attractions under the banner of the National Association for Research and Therapy of Homosexuality (NARTH). Activists very quickly joined together with the national organizations and began their assault on NARTH. The name-calling began and threats were many, including the denial of NARTH members to speak at national conventions. Proposals for open discussions at national meetings were summarily dismissed. Presidents of the national organizations repeatedly refused to provide an audience to NARTH professionals, even though many of these professionals were long time members of the national associations. In Los Angeles, a hotel was forced to cancel a NARTH conference the day it was being held because of activist threats in spite of the hotel having accepted a deposit check many months earlier. Activists threatened to disrupt NARTH meetings. The Los Angeles city council led by activists condemned NARTH meetings. Protests occurred wherever NARTH meetings were held. NARTH was forced to hire extra security to ensure that their meetings were not interrupted. Yet NARTH, a scientific organization, convenes yearly in a convention to present scientific papers and have discussions about providing psychological care to this patient population. Keynote addresses have been given by former leaders of the American Psychological Association including Dr. Robert Perloff, Dr. Nicholas Cummings, and Dr. Rogers Wright. Plenary addresses and workshops have been given by some of the most prominent scholars in the world including Dr. Gerard van den Aardweg of the Netherlands and Dr. Peet Botha of South Africa as well as psychiatrists Richard Fitzgibbons and Jeffrey Satinover. Columnist Cal Thomas has given a luncheon address, and Michael Novak is scheduled to provide a luncheon address this year (2008). Indeed NARTH members are beginning to make a difference as they clarify what science can and cannot say about homosexuality.

Many of these NARTH professionals continue their affiliation with the national mental health organizations and have been active participants in NARTH as well. NARTH members regularly express concern about the activism masqueraded as science in the national mental health organizations and have found support from colleagues who have been very critical of some of the position statements and resolutions issued by the national organizations that represent little more than activist notions. What's even more astounding is that NARTH scientists are beginning to find venues for their research in peer-reviewed journals and public arenas. It appears that both the profession and the public are indeed tired of the activism surrounding this issue, and those on both sides of this political issue are calling for more dialogue and less activism.

Activism supplanting science has been severely criticized by a number of important mental health professionals including prominent members of the American Psychological Association. In 2005, Rogers Wright, a former member of APA's board of directors, and Nicholas Cummings, a former president of the APA, recently made activists' intimidation and harassment public. In their book, *Destructive Trends in Mental Health*, they describe the politics and activism surrounding the decision to declassify homosexuality:

> The Diagnostic and Statistical Manual of the American Psychiatric Association yielded suddenly and completely to political pressure in 1973 when it removed homosexuality as a treatable aberrant condition. A political firestorm had been created by gay activists within psychiatry, with intense opposition to normalizing homosexuality coming from a few outspoken psychiatrists who were demonized and even threatened, rather than scientifically refuted.
>
> Psychiatry's House of Delegates sidestepped the conflict by putting the matter to a vote of the membership, marking the first time in the history of healthcare that a diagnosis or lack of diagnosis was decided by popular vote rather than scientific evidence.[57]

Cummings and Wright concluded that the national mental health organizations had established precedents that "medical and psychological diagnoses are subject to fiat." Cummings and Wright noted that "APA has chosen ideology over science, and thus diminished its influence on the decision-makers in our society."[58]

Of greater concern are the activists' attempts in the national associations to ban psychological care for those distressed by unwanted homosexual attractions. Former APA president Dr. Robert Perloff has taken a particularly strong stand against such efforts. He noted that "if homosexuals choose to transform their sexuality into heterosexuality, that resolve and decision is theirs, and theirs alone and should not be tampered with by any special interest group—including the gay community."[59] He continued, "To discourage a psychotherapist from undertaking a client wishing to convert is . . . anti-research, anti-scholarship, and antithetical toward the request for truth."[60]

It is interesting to note that Dr. Perloff was the recipient of an award given by Division 44 of the APA (this is the division of gay and lesbian psychologists). Even this distinguished scientist, who has been an ardent supporter of gay rights, was threatened when he gave the keynote address at a NARTH conference. Prior to giving the address, Dr. Perloff received a warning call from a former member of APA's board of directors. The caller told Dr. Perloff that a group of APA members was deeply concerned that he had the audacity and political incorrectness to address NARTH (defined as "a bunch of bad guys"). Dr. Perloff's response to the caller was, "If APA or any of its special interest mafias seek to bring ethics charges against me, they will face litigation the likes of which they have never encountered before."[61]

The American Psychological Association has come very close to ratifying a statement that would declare therapy to modify sexual orientation unethical. Fueled by activist agendas and not scientific data, the APA rejected the ban with a very narrow margin. It was Dr. Perloff who persuaded APA's board of directors to place science and professional practice above activism, calling attention to the ethical principle of client autonomy and client self-determination. Dr. Perloff insisted that self-identified homosexuals had a right to psychological care aimed at modifying unwanted sexual attractions.[62] In response to attempts to ban psychological care for unwanted homosexuality, Dr. Nicholas Cummings asked "why does free choice go only one way?"[63]

It was in this context of banning the treatment for unwanted homosexuality that another kind of activism emerged—protests from ex-gays. In 2000, the American Psychiatric Association was poised to ban such treatments, but their meeting in Chicago was greeted with busloads of ex-gays, many from religious organizations. They carried signs that focused on client autonomy, client self-determination, and their right to choose psychological care for unwanted homosexual attractions. Dr. Robert L. Spitzer, the psychiatrist who led the charge to remove homosexuality from the psychiatric manual in 1973, walked out to meet with members of some of the groups. I accompanied him. He listened intently to some of the stories of how these individuals had changed, and they sounded credible to him. He wondered whether what he and other members of the mental health profession and the lay public had been led to believe (namely, that homosexual orientation was fixed and unchangeable) was actually true. As an international expert in conducting such research, he decided that he could do a study to see if individuals could actually change.

Though somewhat skeptical of Spitzer's intentions considering his history of supporting gay causes, after much discussion I, along with others, decided to trust Spitzer's integrity as a scientist and provided him with two hundred former patients who had changed from a homosexual orientation to a heterosexual orientation and who reported this sustained change for at least five years. Spitzer completed his study, adhering to the highest standards of research and eliminating virtually any bias through a system of interrater scoring (a method of using independent evaluators to support interview results).

To Spitzer's admitted surprise, he found that 66 percent of the men and 44 percent of the women had achieved good heterosexual functioning. He also concluded that 89 percent of the men and 95 percent of the women were bothered slightly or not at all by unwanted homosexual attractions. Contrary to assertions that reorientation therapy was potentially harmful, he did not find this to be the case at all. Many of the participants in his study were depressed when they began psychological care. Almost none were depressed at its termination. Spitzer concluded that changes were made not just in behavior but also in core features of sexual orientation including attraction and fantasy.[64]

Spitzer's research demonstrated that, contrary to beliefs of the prevailing climate, the data on homosexuality is far from complete. From his research, Spitzer concluded, "Like most psychiatrists, I thought that homosexual behavior could be resisted, but sexual orientation could not be changed. I now believe that is untrue—some people can and do change."[65]

Spitzer's research caused a firestorm of controversy, and he received harassment, threats, and hate mail from a number of sources. This prominent psychiatrist, who remains a supporter of gay rights and gay causes, was labeled "an over-the-hill stage horse galloping toward the limelight, or a court jester hoodwinked by a scheming religious right."[66] Some venues such as the *Journal of the American Medical Association* refused publication of his study. However, after rigorous peer review, his study was found to have merit, and it was published in one of the most prestigious peer-reviewed journals in the world, *Archives of Sexual Behavior*. The study was published amidst the harshest commentaries I have ever witnessed. Though Spitzer's research was rigorously reviewed and found worthy to be published, activists continued to attack Spitzer personally. There were virtually no attempts to refute his research. Consider some of the published reviews of his study.

> "Spitzer's article, for all of its dignified-looking data, scientific journal format, and partial disclaimers, is in essence irresponsible and unscientific."[67]

"Spitzer's study is methodologically flawed and disturbingly silent about ethical concerns. It is disappointing that the *Archives* elected to publish it."[68]

"There are substantial dangers involved in the publication of Spitzer's article because of the politically charged atmosphere within which the findings and conclusions are presented."[69]

A group of fourteen scientists deemed that even the publication of the study caused harm and violated the Nuremberg Code! The authors of this critique noted that the consequence of Spitzer's study would be that "homophobic and heterosexist audiences will use it to further their agendas."[70]

Attacks were aimed at Spitzer for conducting the research, and accusations of causing harm by even conducting the study were many, but there was virtually no legitimate criticism of the research itself. By any standard, Spitzer's research was considered to be of the highest quality for the methods he used. Essentially the conclusions that he reached were unassailable. Spitzer allowed those who formerly struggled with unwanted homosexuality to speak for themselves in the pages of one of the most prominent peer-reviewed journals in the world. Had Spitzer conducted the study with any other group, there very likely would have been no criticism, and his research would have encountered little opposition. Spitzer's other publications attest to this fact.

Activists continue to rant and suggest that there is no need to study change from homosexuality, and that research on the subject will cause harm to self-identified homosexuals. In spite of a political climate where activism often trumps science, and activist claims go uncritically examined, there is no rational basis for the speculation that studying homosexuality will harm gay-identified individuals. J. Michael Bailey noted, "It is difficult to argue that good scientific studies, or rational, open discussion will harm individuals."[71]

In this instance, the scientific peer-review system prevailed, and the Spitzer study was published. Spitzer's friends quickly became his critics, and he was attacked by the both the gay press and the academy. In spite of the attacks, Spitzer, who continues to support gay rights, declared that "science progresses by asking interesting questions, not by avoiding questions whose answers might not be helpful in achieving a political agenda."[72]

There were few scientists who dared to provide an academic review of Spitzer's study. One commentary stands out because of its scholarly approach to Spitzer's research. As part of the agreement with those who assisted him by providing former patients, Dr. Spitzer consented to make his data available for scrutiny by other scientists. Dr. Scott Hershberger, a distinguished scholar and statistician who is also a self-identified essentialist (one who believes that homosexuality is biologically determined and who is very supportive of gay causes) elected to accept Spitzer's offer, ostensibly to find fatal flaws in the study.

Hershberger elected to subject the Spitzer study to a Guttman analysis, thus further scrutinizing the study. This is essentially a statistical procedure used to determine if the reported changes in sexual orientation occurred in an orderly fashion (actually to determine the veracity of the reports made by the participant in the study).

Subsequent to his analysis of the Spitzer study, Hershberger concluded, "The orderly, law-like pattern of changes in homosexual behavior, homosexual self-identification and fantasy observed in Spitzer's study is strong evidence that reparative therapy can assist individuals in changing their homosexual orientation to a heterosexual orientation. Now it is up to those skeptical of reparative therapy to provide comparably strong evidence to support their position. In my opinion, they have yet to do so."[73]

Though Spitzer's study was not the only study to provide support for the change from homosexuality to heterosexuality, his study opened the door for research on homosexuality because it was the largest of its kind. He studied the affective components of the homosexual experience and was considerably more detailed in his assessment than other studies. His study lifted the moratorium on the scientific investigation of homosexuality. The irony, of course, was that Spitzer was the psychiatrist who essentially closed the door on such research in 1973. Spitzer did exactly what he had done in 1973: he challenged the prevailing orthodoxy yet again. In 2003, he challenged the assumption that "every desire for change in sexual orientation is always the result of societal pressure and never the product of a rational, self-directed goal."[74] From his research, he concluded that many participants "made substantial changes in sexual arousal and fantasy—not merely behavior. Even subjects who made less substantial change believed it to be extremely beneficial."[75]

Not only did Spitzer's research provide hope for those who struggled with unwanted homosexual attractions, but it also built bridges to both historical and current studies that demonstrate change is indeed possible. It encouraged researchers and professional therapists to emerge from the academic and professional closets, and once again reclaim their scientific and professional credentials in examining the psychological care of those who were unhappy with unwanted homosexual attractions.

Current Status of Psychological Care for Unwanted Homosexual Attractions

Research on psychological care to help individuals overcome unwanted homosexual attraction is ongoing. Considering the historical research on reorientation therapy, Jeffrey Satinover reviewed a significant number of outcome studies and reported a composite success rate of 50 percent.[76] William Masters and Virginia Johnson, the famed sex researchers, reported a 65 percent success rate after a five-year follow-up.[77] Elizabeth James conducted an analysis of over a 100 studies and concluded that when all of the research was combined, approximately 35 percent of those with homosexual attractions "recovered" with an additional 27 percent "improved." She concluded that significant improvement and even complete recovery (from a homosexual orientation) is entirely possible.[78]

A published study co-authored by myself revealed that 68 percent of the participants perceived themselves as either exclusively or entirely homosexual, and another 22 percent stated that they were more homosexual than heterosexual prior to therapy. After therapy, only 13 percent perceived themselves as exclusively or entirely homosexual, while 33 percent described themselves as exclusively or entirely heterosexual. Ninety-nine percent of the respondents reported that they believed therapy to change homosexual attraction can be effective and valuable.[79] Other researchers report success rates in treating unwanted homosexual attractions varying from 30 percent to 70 percent.

More recent research has identified factors that seem to be important in diminishing unwanted homosexual attractions in those who seek psychological care. In his doctoral dissertation at Fordham University, Elan Karten found that treatment success is best predicted by a reduction in conflict regarding the expression of non-sexual affection toward men. This finding has important theoretical and clinical implications. Perhaps for some boys, early childhood development of strong, non-sexual relationships with other males will prevent the development of homosexuality. In addition, the development of healthy, non-sexual relationships with men is an important part of the treatment process. Additional findings by Karten suggest that homosexual attractions may be more related to gender (a sense of maleness or masculinity) rather than to sexuality itself. Therefore treatment aimed at strengthening gender identity may be very efficacious.[80]

Perhaps one of the more interesting longitudinal studies was conducted by Dr. Stanton Jones, who, along with his co-investigator Dr. Mark Yarhouse, studied whether some individuals can alter aspects of their sexual orientation through religious ministries. Their conclusion: yes. Using well-accepted, standard psychological measures, Jones and Yarhouse found solid evidence that homosexual orientation can be significantly changed through Christian ministry interventions.[81] Such interventions are not so different from those used by members of Alcoholics Anonymous (AA) after the medical community literally gave up on them. Perhaps the comparison is not lost on this population.

Finally, a recent study was published in a peer-reviewed journal, examining client perceptions of how reorientation therapy and self-help groups can promote changes in sexual orientation. Among the factors impacting the change process was that of having a support group, a caring or nurturing therapist, and a spiritual leader. Spirituality was especially noted as important, and those components of spirituality that contributed to change included scripture study; confession to a spiritual leader; faith in God; prayer, which was particularly conducive to inner healing; belief of God's unconditional love, acceptance, and grace; full commitment to God and Christ; belief that God has a plan for that person; the Holy Spirit giving strength, comfort, direction; and God's forgiveness.[82]

Interestingly enough, after years of demonstrating animosity toward religion, the American Psychological Association has begun to offer support for spiritual interventions in psychological care. Psychologists Allen Bergin and Scott Richards have published scientific books under the banner of the APA that address the importance of spiritual interventions.[83] Psychiatrist Richard Fitzgibbons co-authored a signature book on the psychology of forgiveness, again under the auspices of the APA.[84] In addition, the APA has begun to focus on the importance of a client's right to seek psychological care as well as the importance of religion as an aspect of diversity.[85]

In recent months, the American Psychological Association has called attention to the importance of client autonomy, client self-determination, and client diversity (including religious diversity), and in a new pamphlet, it issued the following statement: "Mental health organizations call on their members to respect a person's [client's] right to self-determination."[86] This right included the recognition and role of faith tradition in the lives of those who seek psychological care.[87]

This role of faith tradition and spiritual intervention suggests that homosexuality is not merely a psychological problem but may also be a religious challenge responsive to both psychological care and spiritual interventions.

Homosexuality and Faith Traditions: An LDS Theological Perspective

For centuries Muslims, Jews, and Christians (about half the world's population) have believed that certain actions and behaviors are forbidden by God. These religious believers have maintained the tradition that sex outside of marriage is prohibited and that heterosexual marriage is the ideal adult relationship. These traditional faiths view homosexual relationships as non-life giving and outside the will of God.

In Islam, Allah condemns homosexuality explicitly in the Qur'an: "Do you approach the males of humanity, leaving the wives Allah has created for you? Nay, you are a people who transgress" (Qur'an 26:165–166). Traditional orthodox Muslims generally acknowledge that the Hadith literature contains the authentic sayings of Muhammad. The following statement is found within: "When a man mounts another man, the throne of God shakes."[88] There is no doubt among orthodox Muslims that Allah condemns homosexual behavior.

The Jewish scholar Dennis Praeger noted that "Judaism cannot make peace with homosexuality because homosexuality denies many of Judaism's most fundamental principles. It denies life, it denies God's expressed desire that men and women cohabit, and denies the structure that Judaism wishes for all mankind: the family."[89] Homosexuality is contrary to the Jewish ideal: family life, one of the most distinguishing characteristics of Judaism.

Christianity supports the importance of the male-female design. According to Christian philosopher Gilbert Meilaender, "There should be no discussion of homosexuality that is not also a discussion of marriage and its purposes."[90] Perhaps the noted German theologian Wolfhart Pannenberg stated the Christian perspective on homosexuality the most succinctly: "If a church were to let itself be pushed to the point where it ceased to treat homosexual activity as a departure from the biblical norm, and recognized homosexual unions as a personal partnership of love equivalent to marriage, such a church would no longer stand on biblical ground but against the unequivocal witness of Scripture. A church that took this step would cease to be the one, holy, catholic, and apostolic church."[91]

LDS doctrine on homosexuality, like those of the major world Christian faith traditions, is clear and very compatible with Islam and Judaism in their emphasis on the family and the incompatibility of homosexuality with religious doctrine. With clarity, Church doctrine states, "Homosexual behavior is and will always remain before the Lord an abominable sin."[92] This doctrine is not only based in Biblical history but also in current revelation, a unique characteristic of The Church of Jesus Christ of Latter-day Saints.

The well-known Biblical story relating to homosexual conduct comes near the opening of the Bible in the account of Sodom and Gomorrah.

> But before they lay down, the men of the city, even the men of Sodom, compassed the house around, both young and old, all the people from every quarter: And they called unto Lot, and said unto him, Where are the men which came in to thee this night? Bring them out unto us, that we may know them. And Lot went out at the door unto them, and shut the door after him. And said, I pray you, brethren, do not so wickedly. (Gen. 19: 4–7)

Here, the men of Sodom wish to *know*, or engage in sexual activity with, the men in Lot's house. Lot, however, shuts the door and denounces them for doing wickedly. Because of homosexual acts and other forms of wickedness, God destroyed the city (see Gen 19: 24–25).

This passage of scripture can be reasonably interpreted as an unequivocal denouncement of homosexual conduct that is echoed in many other places throughout the Bible. It is important to know here that the Joseph Smith Translation of the Bible differs from the King James Version (KJV) regarding Lot and his daughters. In Genesis 19:9, the KJV reads, "Behold now, I have two daughters which have not known man; let me, I pray you, bring them out unto you, and do ye to them as is good in your eyes; only unto these men do nothing; for therefore, came they under the shadow of my roof."

The Joseph Smith Translation reads quite differently, "And Lot said, Behold now, I have two daughters which have not known man; let me, I pray you, plead with my brethren that I may not bring them out unto you; and ye shall not do unto them as seemeth good in your eyes." Some employ the KJV to discount the entire story. The Joseph Smith Translation adds clarity and credibility.

As part of the canonized literature for The Church of Jesus Christ of Latter-day Saints, the Bible's pronouncement on homosexual relations is often referenced by Church leaders and is consistent with the Church's position today. For example, the Lord revealed the following to Moses: "Thou shalt not lie with mankind, as with womankind: it is an abomination" (Lev. 18:22, KJV). A footnote clarification reads, "Or with the male you shall not lie as one lies with a woman." In Leviticus, homosexual acts are labeled not only wicked, as in Genesis, but an abomination, a sin that is immoral and loathed by God.

This moral indignation at homosexual acts has logical justification. Two men or two women engaged in sexual activity have no capacity to procreate, one of the fundamental injunctions of the Bible. Marriage is highly esteemed in Christianity. Homosexual marriage is not recognized in the Bible nor is a homosexual union compatible with Christian doctrine.

Church issued statements on homosexuality are not few. Consider the following:

> "Like other violations of the law of chastity, homosexual activity is a serious sin. It is contrary to the purposes of human sexuality (See Romans 1:24–32). It distorts loving relationships and prevents people from receiving the blessings that can be found in family life and the saving ordinances of the gospel."[93]

> "The Lord's law of moral conduct is abstinence outside lawful marriage and fidelity within marriage. Sexual relations are proper only between husband and wife appropriately expressed within the bonds of marriage. Any other sexual contact, including fornication, adultery, and homosexual and lesbian behavior, is sinful. Those who persist in such practice or who influence others to do so are subject to Church discipline."[94]

> "Homosexual and lesbian activities are sinful and an abomination to the Lord (see Romans 1:26–27). Unnatural affections including those toward persons of the same gender are counter to God's eternal plan for his children."[95]

> "Homosexual, including lesbian behavior, is a deviation from divine law in any age regardless of its private behavior, popular promotion, or legal sanction. Society may redefine deviation, but God has not repealed His commandments."[96]

> "Prophets of God have repeatedly taught through

the ages that practices of homosexual relations, fornication, and adultery are grievous sins. Sexual relations
outside the bonds of marriage are forbidden by the Lord.
We affirm those teachings."[97]

"The unholy transgression of homosexuality is
either rapidly growing or tolerance is giving it wider
publicity. If one has such desires and tendencies, he
overcomes them the same as if he had the urge toward
petting or fornication or adultery. The Lord condemns
and forbids this practice with a vigor equal to his con-
demnation of adultery and other such sex acts."[98]

Unfortunately, there are some even within the Church who
have declared that President Spencer W. Kimball's statements
on homosexuality are no longer relevant and have even opined
that this prophet of God was in error. Though Deseret Book
recently published *The Miracle of Forgiveness* again with all of
President Kimball's statements on homosexuality in tact, such
rhetoric questioning President Kimball's prophetic statements
still persists. Some of the activist attempts to discredit and de-
mean President Kimball's statements are blatant and labeled his
prophetic writings homophobic; other attempts are cleverly dis-
guised. In fact, in a recent "compendium" acclaimed by a number of individuals as a great resource on "belief, doctrine and
morals" of the Church, the statements on homosexuality were
entirely omitted.[99] Claiming the book to be a compendium of
Church doctrine on matters of morality, the author included
the following single statement suggesting that it was represen-
tative of the Church's position on homosexuality: "The Church
does not have a position on the causes of . . . susceptibilities
or inclinations . . . related to same-gender attraction. Those
are scientific questions—whether nature or nurture—those are
things that the Church doesn't have any position on."[100]

The author ostensibly intended for readers to believe that the most concise, the most comprehensive, and the most essential First Presidency statement on homosexuality is limited to one that states the Church has taken no position on the genesis of same-gender attraction. A closer examination of the statement demonstrates quite clearly that the author distorted the statement with the intent to promote an agenda. I am not aware of any positions The First Presidency has taken on the causes of any challenges, regardless of what they may be. In fact, that is the full point of the edited comment included in the compendium. By examining the full, original statement by Elder Dallin H. Oaks, one can clearly see the way in which the compendium's author distorted the statement. The statement in full reads, "The Church does not have a position on the causes of *any of these* susceptibilities or inclinations, *including those* related to same-gender attraction. Those are scientific questions—whether nature or nurture—those are things the Church doesn't have a position on."[101]

This is a follow-up response to clarify a statement saying that the Church views same-gender attraction in the same way as any other susceptibility or inclination. The omission of the italicized words together with the exclusion of the many Church-issued statements on homosexuality calls into question the author's motives for writing such a compendium. Indeed, one can reasonably question whether the book is a compendium at all.

Such cleverness is not so uncommon among Church members who disagree with Church doctrine and write treatises to deceive. For a full discussion of this particular compendium ("Uncovering a Wolf in Sheep's Clothing? A Brief Review of Statements of the LDS First Presidency: A Topical Compendium") and other writings, I refer the reader to www.ldsfair. org, an apologetic Web site.

Lest anyone doubt that President Kimball's words are still relevant, the following quote from the 2006 Melchizedek Priesthood and Relief Society manual, which was endorsed by the First Presidency, will serve to remove those doubts:

> If one has [homosexual] desires and tendencies, he overcomes them the same as if he had the urge toward petting or fornication or adultery. The Lord condemns and forbids this practice with a vigor equal to his condemnation of adultery and other such sex act . . . Again, contrary to the belief and statement of many people, this [practice], like fornication, is overcomable and forgivable, but again, only upon a deep and abiding repentance, which means total abandonment and complete transformation of thought and act. The fact that some governments and some churches and numerous corrupted individuals have tried to reduce such behavior from criminal offense to personal privilege does not change the nature nor seriousness of this practice. Good men, God-fearing men everywhere denounce the practice as being unworthy of sons and daughters of God, and Christ's church denounces it and condemns it. . . . This heinous homosexual sin is of the ages. Many cities and civilizations have gone out of existence because of it.[102]

The statements given by modern church leaders mirror the Biblical roots of homosexual conduct's place as sin. That homosexual activity is sinful has been reiterated by both historical and modern-day prophets and continues to be supported full force.

While the current controversy seems to involve a discussion between what science can or cannot say about homosexuality versus what faith traditions or religion say or do not say about homosexuality, the secular argument concerning the immorality of homosexuality is lost. A Kantian argument can be made that homosexual acts violate the categorical imperative. Wright and Cummings offer the following Kantian argument:

> A second *crimen carnis contra naturam* (immoral acts against our animal nature) is intercourse between sexual *homogenii,* in which the object of sexual impulse is a human being but there is homogeneity instead of heterogeneity of sex, as when a woman satisfies her desire with a woman, or a man with a man. This practice too is contrary to the ends of humanity; for the end of humanity in respect of sexuality is to preserve the species without debasing the person; but in this instance the species is not preserved (as it can be by a *crimen carnis secundum naturam*), but the person is set aside, the self is degraded below the level of the animals, and humanity is dishonored.[103]

Kant's categorical imperative is "Act only according to that maxim whereby you can at the same time will that it become universal law." In other words, what if everybody engaged in homosexual acts? What are the consequences for society?

The notion that somehow homosexuality is a "normal" variant of human sexuality is also contradicted by the natural law argument: normal is that which functions according to its design. One could hardly make a logical argument that homosexual anal intercourse between two men functions according to design. In fact, Dr. John Diggs vividly demonstrates in both his written papers and visual presentations the distinct differences between heterosexual intercourse and homosexual intercourse. The former functions according to its design; the latter does not.[104]

Wright and Cummings note, "This argument based on a natural law account of ethics, and similar natural law arguments concerning the immorality of homosexuality are given by Plato's laws and Aquinas . . . and by more modern ethicists such as Ruddick."[105]

They further observe:

> Utilitarian arguments can reach similar conclusions

concerning the moral impermissibility of homosexuality if we postulate that the net effects of homosexual practices (e.g., failure to reproduce, increasing exposure to social sanctions, increased health risks especially in the time of AIDS, etc.) are negative relative to the positive consequences of homosexuality and relative to the net effects of heterosexual practices.[106]

Interestingly enough, the developmental biologist from Brown University, Dr. Anne Fausto-Sterling, a self-identified lesbian, invokes ethics and morality when making a similar point about homosexuality. Referring to the biological argument that often serves as the basis for civil rights of homosexuals (such as marriage and adoption), she notes, "It provides a legal argument that is, at this moment, actually having some sway in court. For me, it's a very shaky place. It's bad science and bad politics. It seems to me that the way we consider homosexuality in our culture is an ethical and moral question."[107]

It is the false notion that homosexuality is an innate, immutable trait that has fueled the argument for same-sex marriage and adoption by same-sex couples.

Homosexuality and Marriage

John Locke noted,

> Conjugal society is made by a voluntary compact between a man and a woman; and tho' it consists chiefly in such a communion and right to one another's bodies and is necessary to its chief end, procreation; yet it draws with it mutual support and assistance, and a communion of interests too, as necessary not only to write their care and affection, but also necessary to their common offspring, who have a right to be nourished, and maintained by them, till they are able to provide for themselves.[108]

In this brief summary, Locke provides a succinct case for why marriage between a man and a woman is good for society: it not only benefits each complementary partner in the marriage but offers the best possible environment for children and for society.

Traditional marriage, since time immemorial, has contributed to the healthy development of men and women and provided an optimal environment for raising children. The benefits of this family structure find much support in the scientific literature. The health and well-being of adults is an important consideration in marriage. When married men and women are compared to cohabitating men and women, researchers have found that married men and women are more financially stable, more apt to own a home, and more apt to accumulate assets in general. The income of married men when compared to single men is significantly higher even when considering professional/educational background and experience.[109]

Married men and women live longer and have fewer mental and physical diseases. Married men and women are more likely to encourage spouses to seek medical care. Adult maturity and fidelity, which is correlated with marriage, provides motivation for men and women to avoid risky health behaviors such as alcohol and drug abuse as well as promiscuous sexual behaviors. The emotional and social support that marriage provides helps individuals cope with stressors, thus providing some protection against both physical and mental diseases.[110]

Marriage provides gender-specific benefits for men, and these benefits, in turn, translate into important goods for society. For example, married men are less apt to commit crime. However, it is important to recognize that it is not the institution of marriage that is beneficial to men but rather the gender complementarity nature of marriage that affords the benefit. In other words, it is not marriage that civilizes men; it is women who do. In his longitudinal research, Steven Nock concluded that this effect of stability in men was not simply an artifact of selection but rather the direct result of marriage. Specifically, subsequent to marriage, men's behavior was actually transformed. This transformation in men's behavior actually translated to men working longer hours, spending more time with family and less with friends, frequenting bars less, and attending church more often. It appears that marriage for men is a rite of passage that transitions them fully into the adult world of responsibility and self control.[111]

Women are also benefited by marriage. Single and divorced women are more likely to be victimized by violent crime. Married women are less likely to be abused by a partner than women in a cohabiting relationship. Infidelity is significantly higher in cohabiting couples than in married couples, and it invites serious conflict.[112]

Homosexual relationships differ from heterosexual relationships in important ways. Homosexual relationships are less permanent, and its participants are less monogamous. Monogamy is usually defined as sexual fidelity. Perhaps the most extensive study on sexual fidelity ever done was completed by Robert Michael *et al.* in 1994. They found that the vast majority of heterosexual couples were monogamous while the marriage was in tact. Ninety-four percent of married couples and 75 percent of cohabiting couples had only one partner in the previous twelve months.[113]

An extensive study on homosexuality and monogamy was conducted in 1984 by David McWhirter and Andrew Mattison. The male couple study was designed to evaluate the quality and stability of long-term homosexual couplings. The study was actually undertaken to disprove the reputation that gay male relationships do not last. The authors themselves are a gay couple, one a psychiatrist and the other a psychologist. After much searching, they were able to locate one hundred and fifty-six homosexual couples who had been in relationships that lasted from one to thirty-seven years. Two-thirds of the respondents in the study had entered the relationship with either the implicit or explicit expectation of sexual fidelity. The researchers found that of the one hundred and fifty-six couples, only seven had been able to maintain sexual fidelity. Furthermore, none of those seven couples had been together for more than five years. In other words, these researchers were unable to find a single male couple able to maintain sexual fidelity for more than five years. Heterosexual couples lived with the expectation that their relationship would last "until death do us part," whereas homosexual couples typically wondered if their relationship would last.[114]

McWhirter and Mattison admitted that sexual activity outside the relationship often raised issues of trust, self-esteem, and dependency. However, they concluded that "the single most important factor that keeps couples together past the 10 year mark is the lack of possessiveness they feel. Many couples learn very early in their relationship that ownership of each other sexually can become the greatest internal threat to their staying together.[115] From this study and others, the term "fidelity without monogamy" emerged. Translated this means that contrary to the heterosexual notion that equates fidelity with monogamy, homosexuals don't equate the two.

Moreover, a recent study by Maria Xiridou *et al.* found that homosexual "married" couples had an average of eight partners per year outside the relationship. This study was conducted at the Amsterdam Municipal Health Service indicating that even in a gay-friendly society, monogamy is not the norm for gay couples.[116]

Prior to the AIDS epidemic, Alan Bell and Martin Weinberg reported that 28 percent of homosexual men had more than 1,000 lifetime partners.[117] Reiterating a similar statistic, Michael *et al.* provided a comparative comment: "It is extremely rare for a heterosexual who is not a prostitute to have 1,100 lifetime sex partners, as the average gay man infected with HIV had in the beginning of the epidemic."[118] Subsequent to the AIDS epidemic, homosexual men averaged four partners per month instead of six partners. The Centers for Disease Control (CDC) reported that between 1994 and 1997, the percentage of gay men reporting multiple partners increased from 23.6 percent to 33.3 percent, with the largest increase in men under 25 years of age. [119]

Sternberg reviewed another CDC report and noted that 30 percent of all gay black men were HIV positive. He reported that 46 percent of the men in his study had unprotected anal sex during the previous month, and less than 30 percent knew that they were infected.[120] J. Michael Bailey quoted a 1981 CDC statistic: "AIDs patients with an average age of 35 years reported an average of 60 sex partners per year, or approximately 1000 life time partners."[121] Then Bailey offered the following explanation: "Gay men who are promiscuous are expressing an essentially masculine trait. They are doing what most heterosexual men would do if they could. They are in this way just like heterosexual men, except that they don't have women to constrain them."[122] Bailey later continued:

> Regardless of marital laws and policies, there will always be fewer gay men who are romantically attached. Gay men will always have many more sex partners than straight people do. Those who are attached will be less sexually monogamous. And although some gay male relationships will be for life, these will be fewer than among heterosexual couples. . . The relative short duration, the sexual infidelity—are indeed destructive in a heterosexual context, but they are unlikely to ever comprise a substantial proportion of gay men".[123]

Gabriel Rotello, a gay author, noted, "Gay liberation was founded . . . on a sexual brotherhood of promiscuity and any abandonment of that promiscuity would amount to a communal betrayal of gargantuan proportions."[124] In fact, there is a significant portion of the gay community who question whether adapting to marriage is a betrayal of the homosexual lifestyle itself.

While promiscuity among lesbians is less extreme, an Australian study revealed that lesbians were four and a half times more likely to have had more than fifty lifetime male partners than heterosexual women, demonstrating not only the lack of stability in lesbian relationships but the bisexually-behaving nature of those relationships.[125] Other research has been supportive, indicating that as much as 93 percent of lesbians report a history of having sex with men.[126]

Historical and current research reveals grounds for significant concern about the mental and physical health and probable longevity of homosexual individuals. As a group, those who engage in homosexual relationships tend to have higher mental and physical health risks and potentially much shorter life spans. Research has consistently demonstrated that homosexual practices place individuals at risk for some form of mental disorder such as anxiety, depression, suicidality, and multiple disorders. Studies have repeatedly shown that the risks for mental illnesses remain even in societies where there is a greater acceptance of homosexuality.

In the *Archives of General Psychiatry*, researchers Richard Herrell, Jack Goldberg, William True, Visvanathan Ramakrishnan, Michael Lyons, Seth Eisen and Ming Tsuang arrived at the following conclusion: "Same gender sexual orientation is significantly associated with each of the suicidality measures. . . . The substantial increased lifetime risk of suicidal behaviors in homosexual men is unlikely due to substance abuse or other psychiatric co-morbidity."[127] In other words, sucidality is associated with homosexual orientation and not some other co-existing condition like substance abuse or depression.

In the same journal, David Ferguson, John Horwood and Annette Beautrais reached the following conclusion: "Gay, lesbian and bisexual young people were at increased risks of major depression . . . generalized anxiety disorder . . . conduct disorder . . . nicotine dependence . . . multiple disorders . . . suicidal ideation . . . suicide attempts."[128]

Researchers J. Michael Bailey, Gary Remafedi and Richard Freeman reviewed this research, seeking to discover reasons for these significant differences. They all concluded that there was little doubt a strong association between homosexual practices and mental illness existed.[129]

Bailey in particular offered the following hypotheses for consideration:

- The increased depression and suicidality among homosexual individuals are consequential to society's negative views of treatment of this group.

- Because homosexuality represents a deviation from normal heterosexual development, it represents a developmental error, rendering homosexual individuals vulnerable to mental illness.

- The increased psychopathologies in homosexual people is a lifestyle consequence such as the risk factors associated with receptive anal sex and promiscuity.[130]

Bailey's first hypothesis is quite unlikely because the study was replicated in the Netherlands, arguably the most gay-affirming society in the world, and had similar but more robust results. The researchers, Theo Sandfort, Ron de Graaf, Rob Bijl and Paul Schnabel summarized their research:

> Psychiatric disorders were more prevalent among homosexually active people compared with heterosexually active people. Homosexual men had a higher prevalence of mood disorders . . . than heterosexual men. Homosexual women had a higher prevalence of substance abuse disorders than heterosexual women. . . . The findings support the conclusion that people with same-sex sexual behavior are at greater risk for psychiatric disorders.[131]

There are higher rates of sexual molestation found in the histories of homosexuals than in heterosexuals. Using a nonclinical population, Marie Tomeo, Donald Templer, Susan Anderson and Debra Kotler found that 46 percent of gay men and 22 percent of lesbians were sexually abused as children compared to 7 percent of matched heterosexual men and 1 percent of heterosexual women. Particularly intriguing was the finding that 68 percent of the men and 38 percent of the women did not self-identify as gay or lesbian until after the molestation.[132]

Significantly higher rates of domestic violence have consistently been found among homosexual couples when compared to heterosexual couples. Lisa Waldner-Haugrud, Linda Gratch and Brian Magruder concluded from their sample of 283 homosexual men and women that 47.5 percent of the lesbians and 29.75 percent of the gay men had been victimized by a partner.[133] Lettie Lockart found that 90 percent of lesbians had been recipients of one or more acts of violence in the 12 months preceding the study.[134] Gwat Yong Lie and Sabrina Gentlewarrior concluded that 50 percent of the lesbians in their study had been abused by a partner.[135] David Island and Patrick Letellier noted that the incidence of domestic violence among gay men almost doubled that of the heterosexual population.[136]

Judith Bradford, Caitlin Ryan and Esther Rothblum in their national survey of lesbians, found that 75 percent of the 2,000 respondents had received psychological care, a large number for depression. These researchers also noted a high prevalence of physical, sexual, alcohol, and drug abuse in the lesbian population studied. Twenty percent of those in this sample had attempted suicide during the previous twelve months and more than a third of the sample had been depressed.[137]

The scientific evidence is clear and compelling that homosexual practices place its participants at risk for mental illness but what of medical diseases? The evidence is equally as compelling in this area.

Public heath and medical researchers have produced disease and death data for those engaged in homosexual practices. From their research which was conducted in a major area in

Canada, Robert Hogg and Steffanie Strathdee offered the following summary:

> In a major Canadian centre, life expectancy at age 20 for gay and bisexual men is 8 to 20 years less than for all men. If the same pattern of mortality were to continue, we estimate that nearly half of gay and bisexual men currently aged 20 years will not reach their 65th birthday. Under even the most liberal assumptions, gay and bisexual men in this urban centre are now experiencing a life expectancy similar to that experienced by all men in Canada in the year 1871.[138]

The AIDS epidemic is driven overwhelmingly by behavior, with homosexual behavior as the primary means of transmission in the United States. Of the twenty-four categories of AIDS transmission listed by the U.S. Department of Health and Human Services, male homosexuality occupies the first place.[139] Of the 402,722 cumulative AIDS cases reported through 2004, 55 percent involved a single mode of exposure: men who had sex with men.[140] The sole or potential cause of more than 70 percent of all AIDS cases that have been reported in the United States from the first case through 2004 is male homosexual behavior.[141]

Extensive medical evidence supports greater rates of medical disease among homosexuals. For example, the rate of anal cancer infection in homosexual men is ten times the rate in heterosexual men. Other medical conditions wherein there is an overrepresentation of disease among homosexual males include damaged sphincter tissue leading to incontinence, hemorrhoids and anal fissures, anorectal trauma, retained foreign bodies, rectosigmoid tears, allergic proctitis, and penile edema.[142] A study of cancer incidence among male registered homosexual partners in Denmark likewise showed an elevated risk of cancer incidence when compared to the general population.[143] Lesbians have higher rates of hepatitis B and C, bacterial vaginosis, heavy cigarette smoking, intravenous drug use, and abuse of alcohol.[144]

The June 2003 issue of the *American Journal of Public Health* was devoted to health risks associated with homosexual practices. The following statement peers at the readers from the journal's cover: "I gave my lover everything including HIV. I didn't mean to. We made a mistake. Maybe deep down we felt it would be better if we both had it."[145] Article after article chronicled in the flagship journal of the American Public Health Association provided a bleak picture of homosexuality and HIV/AIDs. Consider the following brief summaries from several of the articles:

Michael Gross's editorial, "When Plagues Don't End," focused on the resurgence of HIV/AIDS among homosexual men in the United States.[146] The highest rates of HIV transmission are among African-American and Hispanic men who self-identify as gay.[147] Gross concluded, "To prevent HIV transmission, we have little more today than we had two decades ago, when it became clear that the virus causing AIDS is sexually transmitted: behavioral interventions."[148]

In his article on "Black Men Who Have Sex With Men and the HIV Epidemic: Next Steps for Public Health," David J. Malebranche addressed risk assessment and risk reduction. Malebranche referenced a recent six-site U.S. metropolitan area study that concluded that 93 percent of African American men who were HIV infected felt that they were at low risk for HIV and did not know they had contracted the virus.[149]

Malebranche's study also contradicted the view that coming out of the closet or disclosing one's homosexuality is associated with improved mental health, responsible behavior, and lower rates of HIV infection. To the contrary, African-American men who disclose their homosexuality have a higher rate of HIV prevalence than those who do not choose to do so (24 percent versus 14 percent). They also engage in more unprotected anal sex (41 percent versus 32 percent) than those who do not disclose.[150]

The title of Michael Gross's second article in this journal comes with an ominous warning, "The Second Wave Will Drown Us." Citing a Center for Disease Control statistic of a 14 percent increase of HIV/AIDs among homosexual men in the United States between 1999 and 2001, he provided data from California and New York (two states that were excluded from the CDC report!), which included unprecedented outbreaks of syphilis and alarming rates of rectal gonorrhea among homosexual men. Gross notes an emerging subculture of "barebacking" (anal intercourse without condoms) among homosexual men.[151] Gross offered an interesting comparison:

"On the same day that seven astronauts and fragments of the vehicle that failed them plummeted to the fields and woods of East Texas, six times as many US MSM [men who have sex with men] became infected. Maybe the number was higher, since it occurred on a weekend; perhaps lower if news of the catastrophe interrupted libidinous pursuits."[152]

"On the basis of CDC estimates of the lifetime expenditures for treating a single case of HIV infection, MSM infections acquired that single day will cost $6.5 million. The cost in human potential need not enter the calculus even for a voodoo economist, unless so muddled by moral outrage that he thinks sex between men is indeed something to 'die for.'"[153]

Perhaps the most alarming study in this journal of American health was that reported by Beryl Koblin *et al.* titled "High-Risk Behaviors Among Men Who Have Sex With Men in 6 US Cities: Baseline Data from the EXPLORE Study." The authors describe the prevalence of risk behaviors at baseline among MSM who participated in a randomized behavioral intervention study conducted in six U.S. cities: Boston, Chicago,

Denver, New York, San Francisco, and Seattle. The data gathered involved homosexual men who were HIV-negative and reported engaging in anal sex with one or more partners during the previous year.[154] The results were staggering among the 4,295 homosexual men: "[Forty-eight percent] and 54.9%, respectively reported unprotected receptive and insertive anal sex in the previous six months. Unprotected sex was significantly more likely with one primary partner or multiple partners than with non-primary partner. Drug and alcohol use were significantly associated with unprotected anal sex." [155]

A final study in this public health journal was conducted by Daniel Ciccarone *et al.* on "Sex Without Disclosure of Positive HIV Serostatus in a US Probability Sample of Persons Receiving Medical Care for HIV Infection," provided additional alarming data to support the conclusion that "risky sex without disclosure of serostatus is not uncommon among people with HIV."[156] The authors of this study concluded, "The results of this study indicate that sex without disclosure of HIV status is relatively common among persons living with HIV. The rates of sex without disclosure found in our sample of HIV-positive individuals translate into 45,300 gay or bisexual men, 8,000 heterosexual men and 7,500 women—all HIV infected—engaging in sex without disclosure in our reference population who were in care for HIV."[157] They later added, "these numbers should be considered a lower-bound estimate."[158]

Of particular concern are the alarming numbers of homosexual men who actually "seek" to become HIV infected. In an article featured in *Rolling Stone Magazine,* the director of behavioral health services for San Francisco County, Dr. Robert Cabaj, told the magazine that at least one quarter of the newly infected gay men may have sought out the fatal disease.[159] According to Gregory A. Freeman, the author of the article, some gay men say being HIV-positive "opens the door to sexual Nirvana" because they need no longer worry about safe sex while others say they can't stand the idea of being different from their HIV-infected lover. The magazine article entitled "In Search of Death," tells the story of Carlos, a man who considers HIV-transmission "the most erotic thing I can imagine."[160] "As sick as it sounds," Carlos said, "killing another man slowly" is exciting."[161]

Called "bug chasing," Dr. Marshall Forstein, the medical director of mental health and addiction at Fenway Community Health, an arm of Beth Israel Deaconess Medical Center that specializes in care for gay and lesbian patients, noted that the phenomenon of intentionally transmitting the virus is growing.[162] Evelyn Ullah, the director of HIV/AIDS in the Miami-Dade County Health Department in Florida agreed. She cited "conversion parties" in the Miami-Dade area, in which the goal is to have HIV positive men infect HIV negative men.[163] Forstein is further quoted as saying, "What frustrates health care professionals the most is that gay men who are doing this, haven't a clue what they are doing. They are incredibly selfish and self-absorbed. They don't have any idea what's going on with the epidemic in terms of the world or society or what impact their actions might have. The sense of my brother's keeper is never discussed in the gay community because we've gone to the extreme of saying gay men with HIV can do no wrong. They're poor victims, and we can't ever criticize them."[164] Forstein concluded, "We're killing each other. It's no longer just the Matthew Shepards that are dying at the hands of others. We're killing each other. We have to take responsibility for this as a community."[165]

Such actions do not bode well for the progress being made in the epidemic. In fact, with the failure of recent vaccines, HIV/AIDS can only be viewed as a behavioral epidemic—one that is poised to cause more destruction as scientists are finding more and more strains of the virus that are resistant to intervention.

The journal's editor summarized, "Having struggled to come to terms with the catastrophic HIV epidemic among MSM in the 1980s by addressing the pointed issues of sexuality and heterosexism, are we set to backslide a mere 20 years later as HIV incidence rates move steadily upward, especially among MSM?"[166]

Does or should such statistics affect adoptive decisions? Are there differences between children who are raised in homes where the parents are homosexual compared to children who are raised in homes where the parents are heterosexual? Does gender matter? Is gender complementarity in parenting important?

Homosexuality and Adoption

The best interest of the child is both the standard in the law and the standard with agencies that provide adoption services. Historically, adoptive couples had to demonstrate that they were physically healthy and emotionally stable and had sufficient longevity to rear a child. The central question was: "Is this family the best fit for the child?" The basic understanding underlying the need for adoption was that some parents were not able to rear the children they conceived or that some children, because of abuse or neglect, needed a home. Such vulnerable children have a right to the best possible parenting arrangement that society can provide, and the best possible arrangement for a child is with parents whose health and lifestyles provide optimal development for that child on his or her journey to adulthood.

Stellar research from the social sciences provides conclusive evidence about the family form that is most advantageous for children: all variables considered, children are best served when reared in a home with a married mother and father. David Popenoe summarized the research nicely by saying, "Social science research is almost never conclusive . . . yet in three decades of work as a social scientist, I know of few other bodies of data in which the weight of the evidence is so decisively on one side of the issue: on the whole, for children, two-parent families are preferable to single parent families or stepfamilies."[167]

85

Children reared in a family with a mother and a father navigate the developmental stages more easily, are more solid in their gender identity, perform better in academic tasks at school, have fewer emotional disorders, and become better functioning adults. This conclusion, supported by a plethora of research studies spanning decades, clearly demonstrates that gender-linked differences in child rearing is protective for children. That is, men and women contribute differently to the healthy development of children.

Diane Baumrind found that children of parents who are sex-typed are more competent. Research has repeatedly demonstrated that the most effective parenting is highly expressive (mothers) and highly instrumental or demanding (fathers).[168] Highly expressive, instrumental parenting provides children with a kind of communion characterized by inclusiveness and connectedness as well as the drive for independence and individuality. These essential contributions that emerge from dual-gender parenting are virtually impossible for a man or woman to combine effectively.[169] Children learn about male-female relationships through the modeling of their parents. Such dual gender relationships provide children with a model of marriage—the most meaningful relationship that the vast majority of individuals will have during their lifetimes.

This gender complementarity is readily observable in differing parenting styles of mothers and fathers. Not only are fathers' parenting styles highly complementary to the styles of mothers, but research also indicates that the father's involvement in the lives of children is essential for optimal child rearing. For example, maternal complementarity is provided by mothers who are flexible, warm, and sympathetic and paternal complementarity is provided by fathers who are more directive, predictable, and consistent.

Alice Rossi's research concluded that mothers are better able to read an infant's facial expressions, handle with tactile gentleness, and soothe with the use of voice. [170] Fathers tend to emphasize overt play more than caretaking. This plays out in various forms among young children and appears critical for later healthy development.

A study authored by Marissa Diener demonstrated that babies (twelve months old) who have a close relationship with their fathers seem more stress resistant than those who did not. Babies who had secure relationships with their fathers used more coping strategies than those who did not.[171] Diener's conclusion has fascinating implications: "there may be something unique to fathers that provides children with different opportunities to regulate their emotions."[172]

Male and female differences emerge in the ways in which infants are held and the different ways in which mothers and fathers use touch with their children. Mothers typically use touch to calm, soothe, or comfort infants. For example, when a mother lifts her child, she brings the child toward her breasts providing warmth, comfort, security, and protection. Fathers, on the other hand, more often use touch to stimulate or excite the child. Fathers tend to hold infants at arms length in front of them, make eye contact, toss the infant into the air, or embrace the child in such a way that the child is looking over the his shoulder. David Shapiro notes that each of these "daddy holds" underscores a sense of freedom.[173]

Researchers like K. Allison Clarke-Stewart reported differences in mothers' and fathers' play. Mothers tend to play more at the child's level. They provide opportunities for children to direct the play or to be in charge, and they often proceed at the child's pace. On the other hand, fathers are more directive, and their relationships with their children look more like a teacher-student relationship, a kind of apprenticeship. Researchers have concluded that the play observed between fathers and children, particularly fathers and their sons, is characterized by a kind of roughhousing. In fact, researchers have so consistently demonstrated this rough-and-tumble play that the acronym RTP appears frequently in the literature to describe this father-child play style.[174]

Clarke-Stewart further noted the benefits from this rough-and-tumble play. This form of fathers' play appeared as an asset to the child's development, extending from the management of emotions to intellectual and academic achievement. A result even more interesting in this form of father's play is related to the development of socially acceptable forms of behavior and does not correlate with aggression and violence but rather correlates with self-control. Children who roughhouse with their fathers quickly learn that biting, kicking, and other forms of physical violence is not acceptable. They learn how to recognize and manage highly charged emotions in the context of playing with their fathers, and such play provides them with opportunities to recognize and respond appropriately to their emotions.[175]

Maternal and paternal approaches to discipline also reflect gender differences. Fathers tend toward firmness, relying more on principles and rules. Mothers tend more toward responsiveness, are more apt to bargain or negotiate, adjust more toward the child's mood and circumstances or context, and seem to more often rely on an intuitive understanding of the child's needs as well as the emotions of the moment. The differences between paternal and maternal approaches to discipline are rooted in the fundamental differences between men and women in their moral senses. Men stress justices, fairness, and duty based on rules while women stress understanding, sympathy, care, and assistance based on relationships.

Researchers have long recognized the critical contributions of mothers to the healthy development of children. No reputable theory or empirical study that denies the critical importance of mothers to the healthy development of children can be found in the professional literature. Recent researchers have concluded that fathers are critical to the healthy development of children as well. Researchers such as Kyle Pruett concluded that infants whose fathers were involved in their early lives (as young as six months) had higher scores on the Bailey Test of Mental and Motor Development.[176] Ross Parke noted that infants whose fathers spent time with them were more socially responsive and better able to withstand stressful situations than infants deprived of substantial interaction with their fathers.[177]

Henry Biller concluded that men who were father-deprived in life were more likely to engage in rigid, over compensatory, masculine, aggressive behavior later. His research, based on more than 1,000 separate sources, demonstrated repeatedly the positive effects of fathers on their children.[178]

A second caretaking female cannot provide this essential fathering. In fact, Sara McLanahan and Gary Sandefeur found that children living with a mother and a grandmother fared worse as teenagers than did those adolescents living with just a single parent.[179]

The negative consequences of father absence either physically or emotionally has been so center stage to children' difficulties that a new term has appeared in the research literature within the past decade: father hunger. This phenomenon seems prevalent in psychiatric clinics where children, especially teenage boys, come for care. Others have noted that this father hunger seems to be the primary cause of the declining well-being of children in our society and is associated with social problems such as teenage pregnancy, child abuse, and domestic violence.[180]

There is emerging evidence that mother hunger also exists. The Eisold report provides evidence that mother hunger may indeed develop when a child is deprived of a mother or mother figure. In the article titled, "Recreating Mother," a male child was conceived by a surrogate mother for two homosexual men. They had arranged an artificial insemination with a woman who agreed to relinquish her parental rights in return for medical care and financial compensation. The child, Nick, was cared for by a hired nanny and began attending school when he was two years old. When Nick was two and a half years old, the nanny's employment was abruptly terminated, another nanny was hired and subsequently fired, and a third nanny was hired. The homosexual couple adopted a second child. At four and a half years old, Nick's behavioral problems resulted in a referral to a female child psychologist, a fourth mother substitute. Because Nick lived in a world where mothers were hired and fired, he fantasized about buying a new mother. Barbara Eisold questioned, "How do we explain why this child, the son of a male couple, seemed to need to construct a woman—'mother'—with whom he could play the role of a loving boy/man? How did such an idea enter his mind? What inspired his intensity on the subject? Eisold sees some normal, innate developmental forces at work in a boy who has no mother. If he has none, he will need to make one."[181]

In spite of the overwhelming evidence supporting the importance of mothers and fathers to the healthy development of children, attempts have been made in the "scientific" literature to blur the lines between the genders and claim that neither mothers nor fathers are essential to the healthy development of children. Such "research" reports have become increasingly bold with their activist agendas.

Perhaps the boldest of such articles appeared in the *American Psychologist,* the flagship journal of the APA, in 1999. In this theoretical article entitled "Deconstructing the Essential Father," the authors argue that neither mothers nor fathers are essential to child development and that responsible fathering can occur within a variety of family structures.[182] As advocates of parenting by homosexual couples, Louise Silverman and Carl Auerbach supported their homosexual parenting theory through their observations of animal behavior. To support their view that parenting by homosexual couples leads to positive child outcomes, the authors cited observations from studies on South American monkeys called marmosets. They noted that "marmosets illustrate how, within a particular bioecological context, optimal child outcomes can be achieved with fathers as primary caregivers and limited involvement by mothers. Human examples of this proposition include single fathers . . . and families headed by gay fathers."[183]

Silverstein and Auerbach concluded from their theoretical view that children, like animals, do not need mothers and fathers, just caregivers. They make no acknowledgement of the unbridgeable differences between humans and animals. They seem to forget that ducks don't date, pigs don't fall in love, and fruit flies don't go to church!

To their credit, Silverstein and Auerbach offer the following explanation for their views:

> We acknowledge that our reading of the scientific literature supports our political agenda. Our goal is to generate public policy initiatives that support men in their fathering role, without discriminating against women and same-sex couples. We are also interested in encouraging public policy that supports the legitimacy of diverse family structures, rather than privileging the two-parent, heterosexual, married family.[184]

Further the authors stated, "We realize that some of the research we cite to support our perspective will turn out to be incorrect."[185]

In other words, the authors have little concern about what is best for children (the best interest of the child was never mentioned in the article). Neither are the authors concerned about whether their views are supported by science. In fact, they boldly declare their activist agenda. What's even more disturbing is that it appears the APA supports this bold activist agenda since the article was given a prominent place in its premier "scientific" journal.

One might ask, "What do researchers conclude about children raised in families headed by homosexual couples?"

Homosexual Couples and Parenting

First of all, it is important to recognize that there is a dearth of research in the area of homosexual couples and parenting. Most of the research that has been conducted has involved children who were born into heterosexual relationships and who were reared by mothers who later openly declared their lesbianism. A smaller group of studies focuses on children of lesbians who became parents through artificial insemination. An even smaller group of studies focuses on children raised by gay fathers. This latter group is so small that it is virtually impossible to even offer commentary.

A closer scrutiny of the available studies reveals an activist agenda not so different from Silverstein and Auerbach's article noted above. In fact, in some cases it appears that the authors' attempt to cover the flaws in the research was revealed upon re-analysis. Though research continues to be trusted to provide serious answers to questions even in controversial areas, it is quite remarkable how many authors note the limitations of their studies quite accurately and then ignore the weaknesses of their studies. They then proceed to provide the readers with firm conclusions for which there is little if any real scientific support.

The activism of the researchers in this area is perhaps best characterized by the efforts of Charlotte Patterson, whose studies have been used in court briefs and who authors publications for the American Psychological Association. Patterson, who is a self-identified lesbian, provided testimony in a Florida court regarding the adoption of children by homosexual couples. Her research was questioned and subsequently excluded. In the words of the Florida court:

> Dr. Patterson's impartiality also came into question when prior to trial, she refused to turn over to her own attorneys copies of documentation utilized by her in her studies. This court ordered her to do so (both sides having stipulated to the Order), yet she unilaterally refused despite the continued efforts on the part of her attorneys to have her do so. Both sides stipulated that Dr. Patterson's conduct was a clear violation of this Court's order. Her attorneys requested that sanctions be limited to the exclusion of her personal studies at trial and this Court agreed to do so. Dr. Patterson testified as to her own lesbian status and the Respondent maintained that her research was possibly tainted by her alleged use of friends as subjects for her research. This potential was given more credence than it should have been by virtue of her unwillingness to provide the Respondent as well as the Petitioner, with the documents ordered to be produced.[186]

In reviewing the research on homosexual couples and adoption, Robert Lerner and Althea Nagai conducted a thorough evaluation of the studies available and offered the following conclusion:

> The claim has been made that homosexual parents raise children as effectively as married biological parents. A detailed analysis of the methodologies of the 49 studies, which are put forward to support this claim, shows that they suffer from severe methodological flaws. In addition to their methodological flaws, none of the studies deals adequately with the problem of affirming the null hypothesis, of adequate sample size, and of spurious correlation.[187]

This critique of the research on homosexual parenting is essentially supported by Dr. Richard Williams[188] of Brigham Young University, who independently arrived at the same conclusion. However, Williams went a step further. He reviewed the follow-up studies of several researchers who had declared that there were no significant differences between children raised in heterosexual versus homosexual families. Williams examined the follow-up studies of the Susan Golombok *et al.*[189] and the Susan Golombok and Fiona Tasker[190] research, which followed the children raised by lesbian parents into adulthood. He noted that the children raised by lesbian parents were more likely to have both considered and actually engaged in homosexual relationships, a point not mentioned by the researchers. This finding is important because many individuals who identify as gay or lesbian early engage in high-risk behaviors.

Richard Williams also re-analyzed the studies from other authors as well. For example, a re-analysis of the Huggins data[191] revealed a significant difference between self-esteem measures of children raised in heterosexual versus homosexual families. The former scored higher on measures of self-esteem. Williams discovered that Charlotte Patterson[192] left unreported similar results. Also, Williams noted that Lewis[193] found but left unreported social and emotional difficulties in the lives of children raised by homosexual couples.[194]

Perhaps the most significant study to be published within the past few years came from Judith Stacey and Timothy Biblarz.[195] They conducted a meta-analysis (a meta-analysis simply refers to the combining of several studies that allows the researchers more confidence in making observations or reaching conclusions) that contradicted nearly twenty years of research purporting that there were no differences between children reared by heterosexual and homosexual couples. The researchers found that the authors' interpretation of their own research was in direct opposition to their data.

Consider the data from their research:

- Based on sex-typed cultural norms, daughters of lesbian mothers when compared with daughters of heterosexual mothers more frequently dress, play, and behave in gender-nonconforming ways.

- Sons of lesbian mothers behave in less traditionally masculine ways in terms of aggression and play. They were apt to be more nurturing and affectionate than their counterparts in heterosexual families.

- A significantly greater proportion of young adult children reared by lesbians had engaged in homosexual behaviors (six of twenty-five) when compared to those raised by heterosexual mothers (none of twenty).

- Children raised by lesbian mothers were more likely to consider a homosexual relationship.

- Teenage and young adult girls raised by lesbian mothers were more sexually adventurous and less chaste than girls reared by heterosexual mothers. Sons were less sexually adventurous and more chaste than boys reared by heterosexual mothers.[196]

Stacey and Biblarz concluded that "the adolescent and young adult girls raised by lesbian mothers appear to have been more sexually adventurous and less chaste . . . in other words, once again, children (especially girls) raised by lesbians appear to depart from traditional gender-based norms while children raised by heterosexual mothers appear to conform to them."[197] Conclusions that there are "no differences" in children raised by lesbian mothers versus heterosexual mothers can only be taken to mean that there were no differences the authors considered important.

The research can be summarized as follows: lesbian mothers have a feminizing effect on their sons and a masculinizing effect on their daughters, suggesting a strong element of learned behavior and preferences. The larger, more important question to be asked is, "How healthy is the rejection of gender roles? What is the impact of such gender confusion on normal gender development?"

Gender nonconformity is the only factor in the literature that predicts future homosexuality. Indeed, the relationship of gender nonconformity to later homosexuality is probably the one of the few areas where George Rekers, an advocate for traditional families, and Dean Hamer, an advocate for non-traditional families, can agree. Rekers stated that "gender nonconformity in childhood may be the single common observable factor associated with homosexuality."[198] Dean Hamer agreed, "Most gay men were sissies as children. Despite the provocative and politically incorrect nature of that statement, it fits the evidence. In fact, it may be the most consistent, well-documented and significant finding in the entire field of sexual-orientation research and perhaps in all of human psychology."[199]

Though the evidence is far from complete, there are sufficient studies to warrant concern. While self-identified gay and lesbian individuals do parent, it is most often after children are conceived in heterosexual relationships. The deliberate creation of motherless or fatherless families, as demonstrated by the research included in this book, poses significant and increased risks for children and society in general.

Conclusion

Sexual relationships, once considered a private matter between consenting adults, can no longer be viewed as such. In fact, Elder James E. Faust summed this point nicely by saying,

> "First, adults need to understand, and our children need to be taught, that private choices are not private: they all have public consequences. . . . It is simply not true that our private conduct is our business. Our society is the sum total of what millions of individuals do in their private lives. That sum total of private behavior has worldwide public consequences of enormous magnitude. There are no completely private choices."[200]

Perhaps there is no better support for Elder Faust's statement than the status of homosexuality in our current American and world culture. No longer is homosexuality just a matter of behavior between consenting adults. There are implications for individuals, for marriages, and even for the redefinition of family life, particularly for children.

Someone once said that science is relative forever but that God is the same yesterday, today, and tomorrow. On the matter of homosexuality, science, major faith traditions, and philosophers agree: whether one believes in a creator's divine design, the impersonal theory of evolution, or the secular argument for the survival of the species, homosexuality is maladaptive, and with maladaptations come risk factors for physical disease and mental illness. In the case of homosexuality, the evidence speaks for itself, and that evidence encompasses truths from science, faith traditions, and natural law. Elder Russell M. Nelson wisely noted, "In the Church, we embrace all truth, whether it comes from the scientific laboratory or the revealed word of the Lord."[201] It is interesting that in this same address, Elder Nelson lauds Immanuel Kant's unwavering faith in God as well.[202]

Most interesting is that Elder Faust, in The First Presidency's Message, summarizes beautifully what I have included in this book. This beloved apostle stated:

> The Church's stand on homosexual relations provides another arena where we offend the devil. I expect that the statement of The First Presidency and the Twelve against homosexual marriages will continue to be assaulted. Satan is only interested in our misery, which he promotes by trying to persuade men and women to act contrary to God's plan. One way he does this is by encouraging the inappropriate use of the sacred creative powers. A bona fide marriage is one between a man and a woman solemnized by proper legal or ecclesiastical authority. Only sexual relations between husband and wife within the bonds of marriage are acceptable before the Lord.
>
> There is some widely accepted theory that homosexuality is inherited. How can this be? No scientific evidence demonstrates absolutely that this is so. Besides if it were so, it would frustrate the whole plan of mortal happiness. Our designation as men or women began before this world was. In contrast to the socially accepted doctrine that homosexuality is inborn, a number of respectable authorities contend that homosexuality is not acquired by birth. The false belief of inborn homosexual orientation denies to repentant souls the opportunity to change and will ultimately lead to discouragement, disappointment and despair.

Any alternatives to the legal and loving marriage between a man and a woman are helping to unravel the fabric of human society. I am sure this is pleasing to the devil. The fabric I refer to is the family. These so-called alternative lifestyles must not be accepted as right, because they frustrate God's commandment for a living-giving union of male and female within a legal marriage as stated in Genesis. If practiced by all adults, these lifestyles would mean the end of the human family.[203]

In these few paragraphs, President Faust provided the truth from science, the truth from religion, and the truth from Kant's natural law. The warnings that accompany these truths are many and include personal, family, and societal consequences if such relationships are accepted. When this First Presidency message is imbedded in context of the proclamation on the family, the message of the restored gospel comes through very clearly:

1. "Marriage between a man and a woman is ordained of God, and that the family is central to the Creator's plan for the eternal destiny of His children."

2. "Gender is an essential characteristic of individual premortal, mortal, and eternal identity and purpose."

3. "God has commanded that the sacred powers of procreation are to be employed only between man and woman, lawfully wedded as husband and wife."

4. "We affirm the sanctity of life."

5. "Children are entitled to birth within the bonds of matrimony, and to be reared by a father and mother who honor marital vows with complete fidelity.

6. "Successful marriages and families are established and maintained on principles of faith, prayer, repentance, forgiveness, respect, love, compassion, work, and wholesome recreational activities."

7. "Fathers and mothers are obligated to help one an-

other as equal partners."

8. "Disability, death, or other circumstances may ne-
   cessitate individual adaptation. Extended families
   should lend support when needed."

9. "We warn that individuals who violate covenants
   of chastity, who abuse spouse or offspring, or who
   fail to fulfill family responsibilities will one day
   stand accountable before God."

10. "We call upon responsible citizens and officers of
    government everywhere to promote those measures
    designed to maintain and strengthen the family as
    the fundamental unit of society."[204]

Hopefully, these truths will set the record straight on the
matter of homosexuality.

Endnotes

1. Drescher, J. & Merlino, J.P., eds., (2007). *American Psychiatry and Homosexuality*. New York: Harrington Park Press.
2. LeVay, S. (1996). *Queer Science*. Cambridge, Massachusetts: The MIT Press, p. 224.
3. Wright, R. H. & Cummings, N. A., eds., (2005). *Destructive Trends in Mental Health*. Cambridge, Massachusetts: Routledge, p. 9.
4. IBID, p. xiii.
5. IBID, p. xv.
6. IBID.
7. IBID, p.xiii.
8. Diamond, L. M. (2008). *Sexual Fluidity: Understanding Women's Love and Desire*. Cambridge, Massachusetts: Harvard University Press, p. 257.
9. Wright, R.H. & Cummings, N. A. (2005). IBID, p. xv.
10. LeVay, S. (1991). "A difference in hypothalamic structure between heterosexual and homosexual men," *Science* 253, p. 1034–1037.
11. LeVay, S. (1996). IBID, p. 143–144.
12. IBID, p. 144–145.
13. Nimmons, D. (March, 1994). "Sex and the brain," *Discover*, p. 64–71.
14. Sax, L. (2005). *Why Gender Matters*. New York: Doubleday, p. 207–208.
15. Bailey, J. M. & Pillard, R.C. (1991). "A genetic study of male sexual orientation," *Archives of General Psychiatry*, 48, p. 1089–1096.
16. Bailey, J. M., Dunne, M.P. & Martin, N. G. (2000) "Genetic and environmental influences on sexual orientation and its correlates in an Australian twin sample," *Journal of Personality and Social Psychology*, 78, 3, p. 524–536.

17. IBID.
18. Bailey, J. M. (1999). "Homosexuality and mental illness," *Archives of General Psychiatry*, 56, p. 884.
19. IBID.
20. Bouchard, T.J. & McGue, M. (2003). "Genetic and environmental influences on human psychological differences," *Journal of Neurobiology*, 54, p. 4–45.
21. Hamer, D.H., Hu, S., Magnuson, V. L., Hu, N., & Pattatucci, A. (1993). "A linkage between DNA markers on the X chromosome and male sexual orientation," *Science*, 261, July, p. 321–327.
22. Risch, N., Squires-Wheeler, E. and Keen, B. J. (1993). "Male sexual orientation and genetic evidence," *Nature*, 262, p. 2063–2064.
23. Hamer, D. & Copeland, P. (1994). *The Science of Desire*. New York: Simon & Schuster, p. 82.
24. Mitchell. N. (1995). "Genetics, sexuality, linked, study says," *Standard Examiner*, April, p. 30.
25. Hamer, D. & Copeland, P. (1994), IBID, p. 104.
26. Rice, G. A., Anderson, C., Risch, N. & Ebers, G. (1999). "Male homosexuality: absence of linkage to microsatellite markers at XQ28," *Science,* 284, p. 665–667.
27. Byne, W. & Parsons, B. (1993). "Human sexual orientation: the biologic theories reapprised," *Archives of General Psychiatry*, 50, p. 229. Friedman, R.C. & Downey, J. I. (1993). "Neurobiology and sexual orientation: current relationships," *Journal of Neuropsychiatry*, 5, p. 131–153.
28. Friedman, R. C. & Downey, J. I. (2002). *Sexual Orientation and Psychoanalysis: Sexual Science and Clinical Practice*. New York: Columbia University Press, p. 39.
29. Cummings, N. A. & O'Donohue, W. (2008). *Eleven Blunders that Cripple Psychotherapy in America*. New York: Routledge, p. 318.
30. Collins, F. S. (2006). *The Language of God*. New York: Free Press, p. 260.
31. IBID, p. 263.
32. McCabe, L.L. & McCabe, E.R.B. (2008). *DNA: Promise and Peril*. Berkeley: University of California Press.
33. LeVay, S. (1996). IBID, p. 282.
34. Diamond, L. M. (2000). "Sexual identity, attractions, and behavior among young sexual-minority women over a 2-year period." *Developmental Psychology*, 36, p. 241–250.
35. Diamond, L. M. (2008), IBID.

36. Greer, M. (2004). "Labels may oversimplify women's sexual identity, experiences," *Monitor on Psychology*, 35, 9, October, p. 28.

37. Freund, K. (1963). "A laboratory method of diagnosing predominance of homo-or hetero-erotic interest in the male," *Behaviour Research and Therapy*, 17, p. 451–457. Freund, K. (1971). "A note on the use of the phallometric method of measuring mild sexual arousal in the male," *Behavioral Therapy*, 2, p. 223–228.

38. American Psychological Association (1998). "Answers to your questions about sexual orientation and homosexuality," Washington, D. C.

39. American Psychological Association (2008). "Answers to your questions for a better understanding of sexual orientation and homosexuality," Washington, D. C.

40. Greenberg, G. (2007). "Gay by choice?" *Mother Jones*, September/October, p. 60–65, 93–94.

41. Nicolosi, J. (1991). *Reparative Therapy of Male Homosexuality*. Northvale, New Jersey: Jason Aronson, Inc.

42. Bell, A.P., Weinberg, & Hammersmith, S. K. (1981*). Sexual Preference: Its Development in Men and Women*. Bloomington, Indiana: Indiana University Press.

43. Rekers, G. A. (1988). "The formation of a homosexual orientation," in *Hope for Homosexuality*, Washington, D. C.: Free Congress Foundation.

44. Dickson, G. L., Byrd, A. D., Howes, R. & Drake, H. (2006). "An empirical study of the mother-son dyad in relation to the development of adult male homosexuality," *Journal of the Association of Mormon Counselors and Psychotherapists*, 30, p. 48–56.

45. Shrier, D. and Johnson, R.L. (1988) "Sexual victimization of boys: an ongoing study of an adolescent medicine clinic population," *The Journal of the National Medical Association*, 80:11, p. 1189–1193; Johnson, R.L and Shrier, D. K. (1985). "Sexual victimization of boys, "*Journal of Adolescent Health Care*, 6. p. 372-376.

46. Friedman, R. C. & Downey, J.I., (1994). "Homosexuality," *New England Journal of Medicine*, 331, p. 923.

47. Louganis, G. & Marcus, E. (1995). *Breaking the Surface*. New York: Random House, p. 79–80.

48. IBID, p. 79.

49. Evans, F. B. (1996). *Harry Stack Sullivan*. New York: Routledge.

50. Fitzgibbons, R. (1999). "The origins and therapy of same-sex attraction disorder," in *Homosexuality and American Public Life*, Christopher Wolfe, Ed. Dallas, Texas: Spence Publishing Company, p. 85–97.

51. Bem, D. J. (1996). "Exotic becomes erotic: a developmental theory of sexual orientation," *Psychological Review*, 103, 2, p. 320–335.

52. Byne, W. & Parsons, B. (1993). IBID, p. 236.

53. Diamond, M.L. (1998). *Enriching Heredity: The Impact of Environment on Anatomy of the Brain.* New York: The Free Press.

54. Paglia, C. (1994). *Vamps and Tramps.* New York: Vantage Books, p. 90.

55. Williams, R. (1992). The human context of agency. *American Psychologist*, 47, p. 752–760. Williams, R. (2004). Agency: philosophical and spiritual foundation for applied psychology. In A. Jackson and L. Fischer (ED.), *Turning Freud Upside Down. Gospel Perspective on Psychotherapy's Fundamental Problems.* Provo, Utah: Brigham Young University Press.

56. Wright, R. H. & Cummings, N. A. (2005), IBID, p. xiv.

57. IBID, p. 9.

58. IBID, p. xiv.

59. Byrd, A. D. (2004). "Former APA president supports NARTH's mission statement, assails APA's intolerance of differing views," *NARTH Bulletin*, 13, 3, p. 1–2.

60. IBID.

61. Byrd, A. D. (2004). IBID, p. 2.

62. Perloff, R. (2003) "Moving forward by sticking your neck out," in *Psychologists Defying the Crowd*, Ed. R J. Sternberg. Washington, D. C.: American Psychological Association, p. 174–187.

63. Cummings, N. A. (2005). "The painful education of a well-intentioned APA president," NARTH Annual Conference Reports, Marina Del Ray California, November 11–13, p. 6.

64. Spitzer, R. L. (2003). "Can some gay men and lesbians change their sexual orientation? 200 participants reporting a change from homosexual to heterosexual orientation," *Archives of Sexual Behavior*, 32, 5, October, p. 403–417.

65. NARTH Press Release (May 9, 2001). "Prominent Psychiatrist Announces New Study Results: Some Gays Can Change," Encino, California : www.narth.com. Also in Nicolosi, J. and Nicolosi, L.A. (2002) *A Parent's Guide to Preventing Homosexuality*, Downers Grove, Illinois: InterVarsity Press, p. 140.

66. Besen, W. (2003). "Political Science," *Journal of Gay and Lesbian Psychotherapy*, 7, 3, p. 69.

67. Hartmann, L. (2003). "Too Flawed: Don't Publish," *Archives of Sexual Behavior,* 32, 5, p. 438.

68. Herek, G.H. (2003), "Evaluating intervention to alter sexual orientation: methodological and ethical considerations," *Archives of Sexual Behavior,* 32, 5, p. 439.

69. Worthington, R. L. (2003). Heterosexual identities, sexual reorientation therapies, and science," *Archives of Sexual Behavior,* 32, 5, p. 461.

70. Wainberg, M.L., Bux, D., Carballo-Dieguez, A., Dowsett, G.W., et al. (2003) "Science and the Nuremberg Code: A Question of Ethics and Harm," *Archives of Sexual Behavior,* 32, 5, p. 456.

71. Bailey, J. M. (2003). *The Man Who Would Be Queen.* Washington, D. C.: Joseph Henry Press, p. 115.

72. Spitzer, R. L. (2001). "Psychiatry and Homosexuality." *Wall Street Journal,* May 23.

73. Hershberger, S.L. (2003). "Guttman Scalability Confirms the Effectiveness of Reparative Therapy." *Archives of Sexual Behavior,* 32, 5, p. 440.

74. Spitzer, R. L. (2003). IBID.

75. IBID.

76. Satinover, J. S. (1996). Homosexuality and the Politics of Truth. Grand Rapids, Michigan: Baker Books, p. 186.

77. Schwartz, M.F. & Masters, W. H. (1984). "The Masters and Johnson Treatment for Dissatisfied Homosexual Men," *American Journal of Psychiatry,* 141, p. 173–181.

78. James, E. (1978). Treatment of Homosexuality: A Reanalysis and Synthesis of Outcome Studies," Unpublished Dissertation. Provo, Utah: Brigham Young University.

79. Nicolosi, J, Byrd, A. D. & Potts, R. W. (2000). "Retrospective self-reports of changes in homosexual orientation: a consumer survey of conversion clients." *Psychological Reports,* 86, p. 1071–1088.

80. Karten, E.Y. (2005). " Sexual orientation efforts in dissatisfied homosexual attracted men: what does it really take to change." Unpublished dissertation, New York: Fordham University.

81. Jones, S.L. & Yarhouse, M. A. (2007). *Ex-gays: A Longitudinal Study of Religiously Mediated Change in Sexual Orientation.* Downers Grove, Illinois: InterVarsity Press.

82. Byrd, A. D., Nicolosi, J. & Potts, R. W. (2008) "Client perceptions of how reorientation therapy and self-help can promote changes in sexual orientation," *Psychological Reports,* 102, February, p. 3–28.

83. Richards, P. S. & Bergin, A. E. (1997*). A Spiritual Strategy for Counseling and Psychotherapy.* Washington, D. C.: The American Psychological Association.

84. Enright, R. D. & Fitzgibbons, R. P. (2000). *Helping Clients Forgive.* Washington, D. C.: The American Psychological Association.

85. American Psychological Association (2008). IBID.

86. IBID.

87. IBID.

88. Islam and Homosexuality. Downloaded at http://www. missionislam.com/.knowledge/homosexuality.htm on 4/7/2008.

89. Praeger, D. (1993). "Judaism's Sexual Revolution: Why Judaism (and then Christianity) Rejected Homosexuality." Downloaded from http://www.orthodoxytoday.org/articles2/ PraegerHomosexuality.shtml on 4/7/2008.

90. Meilaender, G. (1999). "Homosexuality in Christian Perspective," From *Things That Count.* Wilmington, Delaware: Intercollegiate Studies Institute.

91. IBID.

92. The Church of Jesus Christ of Latter-day Saints (August 14, 2006), "Same-Gender Attraction." NEWSROOM. LDS. Org. Downloaded from http://www.lds.org/newsroom/issues/ answer/0,19491,6056-1-201-4-201,00.html on 8/21/2006.

93. The First Presidency (2004). *True to the Faith.* Salt Lake City, Utah: The Church of Jesus Christ of Latter-day Saints, p. 30–31

94. "Standards of Morality and Fidelity," First Presidency Statement, issued on November 14, 1991.

95. The Church of Jesus Christ of Latter-day Saints, *For the Strength of Youth* (Salt Lake City, Utah: The Corporation of the President of The Church of Jesus Christ of Latter-day Saints, 1990), p. 15

96. "Same-Gender Marriage," First Presidency Statement, issued on March 10, 2004.

97. *Teachings of Gordon B. Hinckley* (1997). Salt Lake City, Utah: Deseret Book, p. 8.

98. Kimball, S. W. (1980). "Special Message to All Latter-day Saints, President Kimball Speaks Out on Morality," *Ensign,* 10, 11, p. 96.

99. Bergera, G. (2007). *Statements of the LDS First Presidency: A Topical Compendium.* Salt Lake City, Utah: Signature Books.

100. IBID, p. 418.

101. The Church of Jesus Christ of Latter-day Saints (August 14, 2006). IBID.

102. The Church of Jesus Christ of Latter-day Saints (2006), *Teachings of Presidents of the Church: Spencer W. Kimball*, Salt Lake City, Utah: Intellectual Reserve, p. 181.

103. Wright, R. H. & Cummings, N. A. (2005). IBID, p. 79.

104. Diggs, J.R. (2002). "The health risks of gay sex," The Corporate Resource Council, p. 1–16.

105. Wright, R.H.& Cummings, N.A. (2005), IBID, p. 79.

106. IBID, p. 80.

107. Dreifus, C. (2001). "Exploring what makes us male and female," *New York Times*, Science Section, January 2.

108. *Second Treatise of Government*, John Locke (1980) Hackett Publishing, c. VII, s. 78, p. 43.

109. Wilcox, W. B., Blackman, L., Clayton, O., Glenn, N, Malone-Colon, L. and Roberts, A. (2005). *Why marriage matters: Twenty-six conclusions from the social sciences*. New York: Institute for American Values.

110. IBID.

111. Nock, S. (1998). "Marriage as a public issue." *The Future of Children,* 15, p. 13–32.

112. Waite, L. & Gallagher, M. (2000). *The Case for Marriage*. New York: Doubleday, p. 155.

113. Michael, R., Gagnon, J.H., Laumann, E.O., & Kolata, G. (1994). *Sex in America: a definitive survey*. Boston: Little, Brown and Company, p. 101.

114. McWhirter, D.P. & Mattison, A. M. (1984). *The Male Couple*. Englewood Cliffs, New Jersey: Prentice Hall, Inc.

115. IBID, p. 256.

116. Xiridou, M., Geskus, R, de Wit, J., Coutinho, R. & Kretzschmar, M. (2003) "The contribution of steady and casual partnerships to the incidence of HIV infection among homosexual men in Amsterdam," *AIDS,* 17, 7, May 2, p. 1029–1038.

117. Bell, A.P., Weinberg, M. S. (1978). *Homosexualities: A Study of Diversity Among Men and Women*. New York: Simon and Schuster.

118. Michael, R. Gagnon, J. H., Laumann, E.O. & Kolata, G. (1994), IBID, p. 214.

119. Centers For Disease Control (1999). "Increases in unsafe sex and rectal gonorrhea among men who have sex with men—San Francisco, California, 1994-1997." *Mortality and Morbidity Weekly Report*, 48, 3, 45–48. January 29.

120. Sternberg, S. (2003). 1 in 3 young gay black men are HIV positive. February 6, *USA Today*.

121. Bailey, J.M. (2003). *The Man Who Would Be Queen*. IBID, p. 86.

122. IBID, p. 87.

123. IBID, p. 100.

124. Rotello, G. (1997). *Sexual Ecology: AIDS and the Destiny of Gay Men.* New York: Penguin Group, p. 112.

125. Price, J. (1996). "Perceptions of cervical cancer and pap smear screening behavior by women's sexual orientation." *Journal of Community Health*, 2,2, p. 89–105.

126. Ferris, D. (1996). "A neglected lesbian health concern: cervical neoplasia." *The Journal of Family Practice*, 43, 6, p. 581–584. Skinner, C. & Stokes, A. (1996). "A case-controlled study of the sexual health needs of lesbians." *Sexually-transmitted Infections*, 72, 4, p. 277–280.

127. Herrell, R., Goldberg, J., True, W.R., Ramakrishnan, V., Lyons, M., Eisen, S. and Ming, T.. (1999). "Sexual orientation and suicidality," *Archives of General Psychiatry*, 56, p. 867.

128. Ferguson, D. M., Horwood, L.J. & Beautrais, A.L. (1999). "Is sexual orientation related to mental health problems and suicidality in young people?" *Archives of General Psychiatry*, 56, p. 876.

129. Bailey, J. M. "Homosexuality and mental illness," *Archives of General Psychiatry*, 56, p. 883–884. Remafedi, G. (1999) "Suicide and sexual orientation," *Archives of General Psychiatry*, 56, p. 885–886. Friedman, R.C. (1999). "Homosexuality, psychopathology, and suicidality," *Archives of General Psychiatry*, 56, p. 887–888.

130. Bailey, J.M. (1999), IBID, p. 884.

131. Sandfort, T. G. de Graaf, R, Bijl, R. V, & Schnabel, P. (2001). "Same-sex behavior and psychiatric disorders." *Archives of General Psychiatry*, 58, p. 85.

132. Tomeo, M. E., Templer, D.I., Anderson, S., & Kotler, D. (2001). "Comparative data of childhood and adolescence molestation in heterosexual and homosexual persons." *Archives of Sexual Behavior*, 30, 5, p. 535–541.

133. Waldner-Haugrud,, L.K., Gratch, L.V. & Magruder, B. (1997). "Victimization and perpetration rates of violence in gay and lesbian relationships: gender issues explored," *Violence and Victims*, 12, 2, p.173–185.

134. Lockhart, L.L. (1994). "Letting out the secret: violence in lesbian relationships." *Journal of Interpersonal Violence*, 9, p. 469–492.

135. Lie, G.Y, & Gentlewarrior, S. (1991). "Intimate violence in lesbian relationships: discussion of survey findings and practice implications." *Journal of Social Service Research*, 15, p. 41–59.

136. Island, D. & Letellier, P. (1991). *Men Who Beat the Men Who Love Them: Battered Gay Men and Domestic Violence.* New York: Haworth Press.
137. Bradford, J., Ryan, C. & Rothblum, R.C., Edts, (1994) "National lesbian health care survey: implications for mental health care." *Journal of Consulting and Clinical Psychology,* 62,2, p. 228–242.
138. Hogg, R.S. & Strathdee, S. A. (1997). "Modeling the impact of HIV disease on mortality in gay and bisexual men," *International Journal of Epidemiology,* 26, 3, p. 657–661.
139. 2004 HIV/AIDS Surveillance Report, Center for Disease Control and Prevention, Vol 16, at 32, Table 17.
140. IBID.
141. IBID.
142. Diggs, J.R. (2002) IBID, p. 4.
143. Frisch, M. (2003). "Cancer in a population-based cohort of men and women in registered homosexual partnerships." *American Journal of Epidemiology,* 157, p. 11.
144. Diggs, J. R. (2002), p. 6.
145. *American Journal of Public Health* (2003), 93, 6, Cover.
146. Gross, M. (2003). "When Plagues Don't End," *American Journal of Public Health,* 93,6, p. 861–862.
147. IBID.
148. IBID, p. 861.
149. Malebranche, D. (2003). "Black Men Who Have Sex with Men and the HIV Epidemic: Next Steps in Public Health," *American Journal of Public Health,* 93, 6, p. 862–865.
150. IBID.
151. Gross, M. (2003). "The second wave will drown us," *American Journal of Public Health,* 93, 6, p. 872–881.
152. IBID, p. 879.
153. IBID.
154. Koblin, B. A, Chesney, M. A, Husnik, M.J., Bozerman, S. et al. (2003). "High-risk behaviors among men who have sex with men in 6 US cities: baseline data from the EXPLORE study." *American Journal of Public Health,* 93, 6, p. 926–932.
155. IBID, p. 928.
156. Ciccarone, D. H., Kanouse, D. E,, Collins, R. L., Miu, A. ,Chen, J.L, Morton, S.C., & Stall, R. (2003)."Sex without disclosure of positive HIV serostatus in a US probability sample of persons receiving medical care for HIV infections," *American Journal of Public Health,* 93, 6, p. 949–954.
157. IBID, p. 952.

158. IBID.
159. Freeman, G.A. (2003). "In search of death," *Rolling Stone Magazine*, February 6, 1915. Downloaded at http://rollingstone. com//news/story/5933610/bug_chasers on 4/20/08.
160. IBID.
161. IBID.
162. IBID.
163. IBID.
164. IBID.
165. IBID.
166. *American Journal of Public Health.* IBID, p. 860.
167. Popenoe, D. (1996). *Life Without Father.* New York: Mark Kessler Books: The Free Press, p. 8.
168. Baumrind, D. (1982). "Are androgynous individuals more effective persons and parents?" *Child Development*, 53, 44–75.
169. Greenberger, E. (1984). "Defining psychosocial maturity in adolescence," in P. Karoly & J.J. Steffans, eds., *Adolescent Behavior Disorders: Foundations and Temporary Concerns.* Lexington, Massachusetts: Lexington Books.
170. Rossi, A. S. (1987). "Parenthood in transition: from lineage to child to self-orientation," in J.B. Lancaster, J. Altman, A. S. Rossi & L. R. Sherrod, eds., Parenting Across the Lifespan: Biosocial Dimensions. New York: Aldene de Gruyter, p. 31–81.
171. Diener, M. Mangelsdorf, C., McHale, J., & Frosch, C. (2002). "Infants behavioral for emotion regulation with fathers and mothers: association with emotional and attachment quality." *Infancy*, 5, p. 151–172.
172. Broughton, A. E. (2002). "U study says dads are important, too," *Salt Lake Tribune*, April 5, A1.
173. Shapiro, D. (1994). "Letting dads be parents," *Parents*, June, p. 165–168.
174. Clark-Stewart, K.A. (1980). "The father's contribution to children's cognitive and social development in early childhood," In F A Pederson, Ed., *The Father-Infant Relationship: Observational Studies in the Family Setting.* New York: Praeger.
175. IBID.
176. Pruett, K. D., (1987). *The Nurturing Father.* New York: Warner Books.
177. Parke, R. D. (1981). *Fathers.* Cambridge, Massachusetts: Harvard University Press.
178. Biller, H.B. (1993). *Fathers and Families: Paternal Factors in Child Development.* Westport, Connecticut: Auburn House.

179. McLanahan, S. & Sandefur, G. (1994). *Growing Up With A Single Parent: What Hurts, What Helps.* Cambridge, Massachusetts: Harvard University Press.

180. Blankenhorn, D. (1995). *Fatherless America: Confronting Our Most Urgent Social Problem.* New York: Basic.

181. Eisold, B. (1998). "Recreating mother: the consolidation of 'heterosexual' gender identification in the young son of homosexual men," *American Journal of Orthopsychiatry,* 68, 3, p. 433–442.

182. Silverstein, L. B. & Auerbach, C.F. (1999). "Deconstructing the essential father," *American Psychologist,* 54, 6, p. 397–407.

183. IBID, p. 400.

184. IBID, p. 399.

185. IBID.

186. Petitioner v. Floyd P. Johnson., District Administrator, District X, Florida Department of Health and Rehabilitative Services, Respondent, 17th Judicial Circuit in and for Broward County. Case No. 92-14370 (11) July 27. John A. Frusciante, Judge.

187. Lerner, R. & Nagai, A.K., "Out of nothing comes nothing: homosexual and heterosexual marriage not shown to be equivalent for raising children," Paper presented at the Revitalizing the Institution of Marriage for the 21st Century, BYU, March, Provo, Utah.

188. Williams, R.. G. (2000). "A critique of the research on same-sex parenting," In *Strengthening Our Families,* (Ed.) David C. Dollahite. Salt Lake City, Utah: Bookcraft, p. 352-355.

189. Golombok, S., Spencer, A. & Rutter, M. (1983). "Children in lesbian and single parent households: Psychosexual and psychiatric appraisal, *Journal of Child Psychology and Psychiatry,* 24, p.551-572.

190. Golombok, S. & Tasker, F. (1996). "Do parents influence the sexual orientation of their children? Findings from a longitudinal study of lesbian families." *Developmental Psychology,* 32, p. 3-11.

191. Huggins, S. L (1989). "A comparative study of self-esteem of adolescent children of divorced lesbian mothers and divorced heterosexual mothers," *Journal of Homosexuality,* 16, p. 123-135.

192. Patterson, C. J. (1995). "Families of the lesbian baby boom: Parents' division of labor and children's adjustment," *Developmental Psychology,* 31, p. 115-123.

193. Lewis, K. G. (1992). Children of Lesbians: Their point of view, in D. J. Maggiore (Ed.). *Lesbians and child custody:* A casebook (New York: Garland), p. 85-98.

194. IBID.

195. Stacey, J. and Biblarz, T.J. (2001). "Does sexual orientation of parents matter?" *American Sociological Review*, 66, 2, p. 159–183.
196. IBID.
197. IBID, p. 171.
198. Rekers, G. A. (1995). *Handbook of Child and Adolescent Sexual Problems*. New York: Lexington Books, p. 300.
199. Hamer, D. & Copeland, P. (1994), IBID, p. 166.
200. Faust, J.E. (1987). "Will I be happy?" *Ensign*, May, p. 80.
201. Nelson, Russell M. (1984). "Begin with the end in mind," Fireside Address given at Brigham Young University, September 30, p. 5.
202. IBID.
203. Faust, J. E. (1995). "Serving the Lord and Resisting the Devil," *Ensign*, 25, September, p. 2–7.
204. The Family: A Proclamation to the World," read by President Gordon B. Hinckley at the General Relief Society Meeting held on September 23, 1995, in Salt Lake City, Utah.

Author's Biographical Information

A. Dean Byrd, PhD, MBA, MPH is President of the Thrasher Research Fund and a member of the University of Utah School of Medicine faculty with appointments in the Department of Family and Preventive Medicine and in the Department of Psychiatry. In addition, he is Adjunct Professor in the Department of Family Studies, also at the University of Utah. A licensed clinical psychologist, Dr. Byrd received his academic training at Spartanburg Methodist College, Brigham Young University, Virginia Commonwealth University and Medical College of Virginia, Loyola University, and the University of Utah. He has had visiting professorships in Israel (University of Tel Aviv, Hebrew University, Bar Ilan University), Poland (University of Krakow School of Medicine), Democratic Republic of the Congo (University of Kinshasa School of Medicine), and the Ivory Coast (Ivory Coast School of Public Health). Dr. Byrd is the author of four books and more than two hundred total peer-reviewed journal articles (in mental health journals as well as law journals), book chapters, book reviews, and opinion editorials on homosexuality, homosexual marriage, adoption by homosexual couples, and other family related topics. He has served as an expert witness in court proceedings on family related issues both in the United States and abroad.

SETTING THE RECORD STRAIGHT SERIES

MORMONS & MASONS

GILBERT W. SCHARFFS, Ph.D.

MORMONS POLYGAMY

JESSIE L. EMBRY

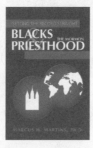

BLACKS THE MORMON PRIESTHOOD

MARCUS H. MARTINS, Ph.D.

EMMA SMITH: AN ELECT LADY

SUSAN EASTON BLACK

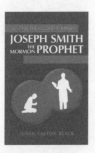

JOSEPH SMITH THE MORMON PROPHET

SUSAN EASTON BLACK

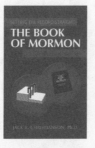

THE BOOK OF MORMON

JACK R. CHRISTIANSON, Ph.D.

THE WORD OF WISDOM

STEVEN C. HARPER, Ph.D.

JOSEPH SMITH: PRESIDENTIAL CANDIDATE

ARNOLD K. GARR, Ph.D.

MORMON TEMPLES

DEAN L. LARSEN

MORMONS & HOMOSEXUALITY

A. DEAN BYRD, Ph.D., MPH

MORMONS & SCIENCE

RODNEY L. BROWN, Ph.D.

MORMON FUNDAMENTALISM

BRIAN C. HALES

To learn more about these and other Millennial Press titles,
visit www.millennialpress.com. Available wherever books are sold.